D0860254

The Impact of
Government Subsidies
on Industrial Management

PRAEGER SPECIAL STUDIES IN
INTERNATIONAL ECONOMICS AND DEVELOPMENT

The Impact of Government Subsidies on Industrial Management

THE ISRAELI EXPERIENCE

Nachum Finger

Foreword by
Seymour Melman

PRAEGER PUBLISHERS
New York • Washington • London

The purpose of Praeger Special Studies is to make specialized research in U.S. and international economics and politics available to the academic, business, and government communities. For further information, write to the Special Projects Division, Praeger Publishers, Inc., 111 Fourth Avenue, New York, N.Y. 10003.

PRAEGER PUBLISHERS
111 Fourth Avenue, New York, N.Y. 10003, U.S.A.
5, Cromwell Place, London S.W.7, England

Published in the United States of America in 1971
by Praeger Publishers, Inc.

© 1971 by Praeger Publishers, Inc.

Library of Congress Catalog Card Number: 71-139883

Printed in the United States of America

FOREWORD

The economic development programs of many governments include subsidy arrangements, especially for industrial investors. Everywhere the assumption has been that industrial operations are thereby undertaken which will have durable economic benefit for a society, and that in the absence of the subsidy systems the new production would be neglected.

This book is, in part, an answer to the question: Do subsidy systems actually operate as a decisive incentive to industrial investment that would otherwise be avoided? Most important, however, this book diagnoses the consequences of subsidy systems in terms of the operating characteristics of the industrial enterprise.

There are two well-known theories and sets of possible circumstances for securing efficient operation of business enterprise. The first is autonomous operation of separate firms combined with relatively free competition in the marketplace. Under these conditions, the more efficient entrepreneurs are rewarded and the incompetent ones are penalized by failure. A second mode of operation is given by the large, central office managed firm. Many sub-enterprises (divisions) are governed by policy-makers in a managerial central office who also police compliance with the policies that they lay down. In this fashion extensive enterprises with as many as 200 sub-divisions can be governed from one central office. Thus U.S. Steel in 1968 had $4,600,000,000 net sales; General Electric, $8,400,000,000; and General Motors had sales of $22,800,000,000. The Gross National Product of Israel in 1966 was somewhat less than $4,000,000,000. Clearly its entire industrial component was only a fractional part of the value product of one of the large U.S. industrial firms.

The subsidy system approach to industrial investment seems to bring about a network of effects that cancel out the efficiency yielding operation of both the independent enterprise system and the central office managed industrial firm.

Mr. Finger has made an important finding in identifying the existence and the characteristics of the "subsidy-maximizing firm." His chapters on this subject are a contribution to economic knowledge and should be an important guide to economists and to government policy-makers.

Students of industrial economy should give close attention to the possible connection between these diagnoses of the subsidy-maximizing firm and the characteristics noted elsewhere of the military industrial firm. Thus the portrayal of the "subsidy-maximizing vs. the profit-maximizing firm" in Chapter 6 of this volume has striking similarity to the contrast drawn elsewhere between the military industrial vs. the civilian enterprise.

Seymour Melman

PREFACE

Subsidies in general, and those provided to manufacturing enterprises in particular, have become accepted tools for the implementation of preferred government policies. Consequently, subsidies are evaluated mainly with respect to their effect on entire systems, be it a nation's economy, a given sector of the economy, or a specific industry. The impact of these subsidies on smaller subsystems such as individual firms, has drawn thus far only limited attention, the assumption being that the theory of the firm remains invariant.

Subsidies not only affect the size of investments, but also alter the basic parameters of design and operation of the industrial firm which further influences practically every major managerial decision. The combined result of all subsidy-related influences on management decisions is not always consistent with, and, in fact, frequently impedes the attainment of objectives set forth by the design of the subsidy system. Evidence of this is the existence of subsidized conventionally nonviable firms, and the occurrence of the continuously subsidized, but, nevertheless, depleting industries.

As a result, it is important that governments, as well as industrial managers, understand the processes leading to the emergence of such firms. The purpose of this book is to analyze some of the elements in this process by examining the impact of government subsidies on three major management decision areas: the financial area, the plant location, and the choice of technology.

The resulting impact of government subsidies on these managerial decisions is the creation of a firm which depends largely on subsidies for its survival. This is a subsidy-maximizing firm, different in goals, methods of operations, and general characteristics from the conventional profit-maximizing firm. The raison d'être of such a firm is the existence of a variety of government subsidy programs. The strategies and tactics employed by managers of such firms, and the recognizable characteristics of these firms are described towards the end of this book.

vii

Awareness of these characteristics may help serve as a yardstick to the government in its overall decision to grant subsidies. Management, on the other hand, can perhaps reflect more intelligently its decision to pursue that road which frequently leads to becoming a subsidy-dependent firm.

ACKNOWLEDGMENTS

I am most grateful to Professor Seymour Melman of the
Industrial and Management Engineering Department, Columbia
University, for his guidance, perspective counsel, and numerous suggestions which have improved the manuscript. My ap-
preciation is also expressed to Professor Lawrence B. Cohen
of Columbia University for his valuable comments and criticism.
Special thanks are due to Mrs. Judith Kaplan for her patient
and careful editing and to Miss Cheryl Jackson for skillfully
typing the manuscript.

Finally, I am particularly grateful to my mother, Mrs.
Mira Finger, my aunt, Mrs. Chaya Solomon, and to Miss
Maya Mosevitzki for being constant sources of encouragement
throughout the preparation of this study.

CONTENTS

	Page
FOREWORD	v
PREFACE	vii
ACKNOWLEDGMENTS	ix
LIST OF TABLES	xv
LIST OF FIGURES	xvii
INTRODUCTION	xix
Methods and Areas of Investigation	xx
Notes	xxii

Chapter

1 COMMON SUBSIDIES GRANTED TO MANUFACTURERS	3
Payments and Services by the Government to the Firm	4
Cash Grants	4
Tax Refunds	4
Loans at Reduced Interest Rates	5
Participation in Work-Force Training	5
Subsidy for the Acquisition of Industrial Land and Buildings	6
Loans for Working Capital	7
Transfer of Equipment	7
Research Expenditures	7
Investment Survey	7
Subsidy Toward Interest Cost	8
Deferment of Fees	8
Remission of Charges	8
Income Tax	8

Property Taxes   8
Indirect Taxes and Charges   9
Investment in Securities   9
Carry Forward Losses   9
Immigrant Investors   10
Accelerated Depreciation   10
Interest on Approved Loans   11
Export Processing Zone   11
Nonquantifiable, Risk-Reducing Subsidies   12
    Subsidies Directly Affecting Management
        Decision   12
    Subsidies Indirectly Affecting Management
        Decision   14
Export Subsidies   16
    Indirect Tax Refund   17
    Refund of Taxes on Raw Materials and
        Intermediate Products   17
    Refund of Dock Fees on Imports for
        Reexport   18
    Property Tax Refund on Equipment and
        Stock   18
    Travel Tax Exemptions for Approved
        Exporters   18
    Financing Export   19
    Transport Services and Insurance   19
    Other Common Incentives Both Quantifiable
        and Nonquantifiable   20
    Notes   24

2   THE FINANCIAL DECISIONS   27

Payback Period   28
Rate of Return on Investment   28
Annual Cost Comparisons--Net Present Value   29
Notes   39

3   THE LOCATION DECISION   41

Site Selection   45
Notes   59

Chapter	Page
4 THE TECHNOLOGY DECISION	60
Notes	73
5 THE SUBSIDY-MAXIMIZING FIRM	74
The Investor	75
The Donor	78
Notes	83
6 CHARACTERISTICS OF THE SUBSIDY-MAXIMIZING FIRM	84
Purpose and Goals	84
Profit	84
Survival	85
Government Relations	85
Managerial and Organizational Characteristics	85
Managers	85
Management Costs	85
Administrative Versus Production Costs	86
Financial Characteristics	86
Capital Structure	86
Loan Guarantees	86
Future Cash Flows	87
Extra Subsidy Financing	87
Return on Equity Investment	87
Capital Budgeting	87
Operational Characteristics	87
Lead-Time for Establishment	87
Plant Location	88
Plant Building and Facilities	88
Process-Technology Characteristics	88
Product Choice	89
Production Run	89
Overall Operational Efficiency	89
Marketing Characteristics	89
Sales Forecast	89
Market Targets	90
Promotion Costs	90
Choice of Projects	90
Environmental Relations	90
Community Relations	90

Chapter   Page

        Government Influence   90
        Government Control   91

BIBLIOGRAPHY   93

ABOUT THE AUTHOR   101

LIST OF TABLES

Table   Page

1   Sample Countries for Subsidy Enumeration, 1966   xxi

2   Rate of Grant as Percentage of Total Investment in Fixed Assets, Israel   4

3   Loans and Interest Rates   5

4   Export Incentives in Israel--Rates of Refund   18

5   Budgetary Industrial Export Subsidies, by Item, 1964-66   20

6   Total Industrial Export Versus Industrial Export Subsidies   21

7   Examples of Subsidy Systems by Country   22

8   Sources for Investment Capital in Manufacturing Industries, Israel, 1960-67   33

9   Non-Equity Capital and Government Grants and Loans as a Percentage of Total Investment, Israel, 1961-67   35

10   Ratio of Equity Capital to Total Balance Sheet in Industrial Companies, Israel and Other Countries   37

11   Investment Approvals in Foreign Currency, Israel, 1962-67   45

12   Approved New and Expansion Projects by Industry Branch, Israel, 1962-67   49

Table   Page

13   Approved Projects in Priority Regions,
     Israel, 1962-67   50

14   Percent Approved Projects in Priority Regions   51

15   Approved Projects by Priority Development
     Region, 1966-67   51

16   Total Investment in Industry by Branch and
     Region, Israel, 1966-67   53

17   Allocation of Investment Capital, Israel, 1967   55

18   Average Monthly Salary and Percentage Change
     in the Average Monthly Salary per Worker in
     Industry, Crafts, Mines, and Quarries, Israel,
     1962-66   62

19   Wages and Salaries in Manufacturing   62

20   Percentage Increase in Wages, Output, and
     Ratio of Capital to Output and Ratio of Average
     Monthly Wages to Output, Israel, 1961-66   63

21   Employment and Output per Worker in Industry,
     Israel, 1950-66   64

22   Index of the Price of Industrial Equipment
     Relative to the Price of Labor, 1962-66   66

23   Electrical Power Consumption by Israeli
     Industry   66

24   Capital Stock per Gainfully Employed Person
     in Industry, Mining, and Quarrying, Israel,
     1950-67   67

25   Approved Capital Stock per Employed Person
     in Industry, Israel, 1963-67   68

LIST OF FIGURES

Figure   Page

1   Schedule of Cumulative Demand for Capital   30

2   Total Investment in Manufacturing,
    Government Loans and Grants to Investment
    in Manufacturing, Israel, 1960-67   34

3   Non-Equity Capital and Government Grants
    and Loans as a Percentage of Total Investment
    in Approved Manufacturing Enterprises in
    Israel, 1961-67   36

4   Approved Investments in Foreign Currency,
    Israel, 1963-67   44

5   Priority Development Areas of Israel   47

6   Approved Development Region Projects as
    Percentage of Total Number of Approved
    Projects, Israel, 1962-67   48

7   The Impact of Subsidies on Break-Even
    Analysis   57

8   Employed Persons in Industry and Crafts by
    Natural and Development Region   69

9   Capital-Labor Proportion in Various Processes   71

10 The Subsidy-Maximizing Versus the
    Profit-Maximizing Firm   80

INTRODUCTION

Subsidy programs are used extensively by governments for implementing preferred policies.

Industrial development, as part of an economic development process, has been one of the focal points of subsidy policies. For the industrial manager, subsidy systems are significant because they alter the basic parameters of design and operation of the industrial enterprise. Every major aspect of engineering economy is affected--from plant location and the selection of preferred equipment to the adoption of plans for depreciation of capital investments. Therefore, the impact of subsidies for industrial development on the design and operation of the firm serves as the subject of this book.

The subsidy idea itself is not a newly developed device or technique to cope with modern economic problems, but rather an outgrowth of similar practices employed in the past. These practices range from early Eqvptian and Greek custom duties, through a variety of Roman and medieval fiscal measures, to the protectionist philosophy of mercantilism and the modern array of subsidy systems. As a result, the word "subsidy" has undergone various changes and adaptations throughout the years, resulting in a variety of meanings.[1]

For the purpose of this book several common definitions were combined to provide an appropriate interpretation of the term. Thus, the term "subsidy" will represent an input or a specific contribution by the government to business costs. It involves the shift of resources from one segment of the economy to another by government decree through (a) direct cash payments, (b) remission of charges, and (c) supply of commodities or services.[2]

The subsidies with which we are concerned are those granted to manufacturing enterprises and which lead subsequently to the emergence of the subsidized industrial firm. Thus far, literature has dealt largely with such subsidy programs from the providers' point of view and with the effect of these programs on the provider (i.e., the government). This book will investigate the effect of subsidy programs from a different perspective, that of the individual firm.

Despite the fact that subsidy programs have become a major factor in the various policy and operational decisions of the firm, it is oftentimes assumed that the conventional theory of the firm as an entity seeking to maximize profits through the efficient combination of production factors remains unchanged. Consequently, it is the purpose of this book to test this assumption through a systematic analysis of the impact of subsidy programs on the behavior and structure of the individual enterprise. This analysis is carried out by evaluating critically the impact of that portion of subsidies which directly impinges on the major industrial management decision areas such as the investment decision, the plant location decision, the technological and other operational decisions. These areas of decision are singled out for our analysis both for their general significance in determining the characteristics of the firm, and because a major portion of industrial subsidy programs are aimed at these aspects of the enterprise.

Do subsidies actually affect these decisions, and if so, in what way? How does the intervention of this factor, the subsidy, influence the established criteria and rules for management decision-making? Is the subsidized enterprise the same as the unsubsidized one in scope, goals, and operational methods?

Answers to some of these questions will be sought in the following chapters, and will help eventually to develop and depict in a systematic way the theory and the characteristics of the subsidy-maximizing firm.

METHODS AND AREAS OF INVESTIGATION

In view of the extensive variety of subsidies employed by governments throughout the world, it appeared necessary to identify, list, and classify the various subsidies whose impact on the management decision process we seek to analyze. For such an analysis to be effective, the subsidies selected must lend themselves to evaluation and observation. At the same time they must be widely applied.

An enumeration and classification of subsidy programs is therefore carried out through the analysis of various subsidies and incentives granted to industrial enterprises in the sample fourteen countries listed in Table 1.

The reasons for choosing these particular countries lie in the wide organic differences in their basic structure. The sample includes both industrially developed and developing

TABLE 1

Sample Countries for Subsidy Enumeration, 1966

COUNTRY	GROSS NATIONAL PRODUCT (millions of dollars)	GROSS NATIONAL PRODUCT PER CAPITA (dollars)
Brazil	25,790	310
China, Republic of	3,138	235
India	36,895	74
Ireland	2,943	1,020
Israel	3,822	1,454
Japan	97,480	986
Korea, Republic of	3,822	131
Mexico	21,770	493
Netherlands	20,750	1,666
Pakistan	13,450	115
Peru	3,547	295
Spain	24,570	771
United Kingdom	105,310	1,924
United States	747,600	3,796

Source: U.S. Arms Control and Disarmament Agency, Economics Bureau, World Military Expenditures and Related Data, Research Report 68-52 (Washington, D.C.: U.S. Government Printing Office, December, 1968).

nations; nations with a high GNP and nations with a low GNP; some with a high per capita income and several with a low per capita income; several with a socioeconomic system which is capitalistic in nature and others somewhat socialistic in nature; some nations with democratic governments and others with dictatorial regimes.

In addition, most countries in this sample have employed the same or a similar type of subsidy programs, and have had at least some limited documentation of these programs.

Israel, a rapidly developing country, is one of the few nations which has systematically experimented with new subsidy systems as well as those employed by other nations. Also, the government of Israel has accumulated and made public relevant data as to the types, magnitude, and results emanating from diverse subsidy programs. In view of this data regarding the formulation and operation of subsidy programs, Israel is an especially fruitful locale for this study. Israeli industrial enterprise includes extensive product variety and is managed by a corps of men skilled in the business process. Thus, for this investigation, Israeli experience is used as a prime source of data.

The enumeration and classification of subsidies in Chapter 1 serves a dual purpose. It groups the various subsidies into categories permitting analysis by accepted engineering-economy criteria, and, at the same time, it helps us identify the particular areas of management decisions upon which these subsidies impinge. These areas are the investment, capital structure, plant location, and technology decisions. Consequently, a chapter is devoted to the analysis of the impact of the various subsidy programs on these managerial decisions. Throughout the analysis, accepted engineering-economy criteria such as the Present Value Method, Break-Even Analysis, the ratio of man-machine costs, and respectively substantiating empirical data are utilized.

Since these three areas of decision-making embody crucial functions of industrial management, the resulting management action is an indication of the individual firm's behavior under the impact of subsidies. This behavior enables us to conclude the investigation with the formulation of a subsidy-maximizing firm concept and the development of this firm's goals, strategies, tactics, and general characteristics as compared to those of the conventional profit-maximizing firm.

NOTES

1. For a summary of "subsidy" definitions see: U.S. Congress, Joint Economic Committee, Subsidy and Subsidy-Effect Programs of the U.S. Government, Joint Committee Print (Washington, D.C.: U.S. Government Printing Office, 1965).

2. Ibid., p. 9.

The Impact of
Government Subsidies
on Industrial Management

CHAPTER **1** COMMON SUBSIDIES
GRANTED TO
MANUFACTURERS

A survey of present day subsidy practices reveals an
ever-growing variety of subsidy programs. In this chapter
those subsidies which directly affect the industrial management
decision process will be identified. This identification is ac-
complished by illustrating the entire spectrum of such subsidies, and by classifying them into groups, thus permitting
observations as to their impact on managerial decisions.

There are two basic types of classification. The first,
and most often encountered in the literature, is a classification
from the providers' point of view, namely, according to government objectives--for example, subsidies for regional development, subsidies for the encouragement of investments, and
export subsidies. The second type of classification is from
the receivers' point of view, namely according to the effect of
subsidies on management. Since the latter classification is
the focal point of this volume, management functions and areas
of decision can be used as criteria for classification.

The following subsidies are drawn from the list of sample
countries described in the Introduction. These subsidies are
divided into four categories which allow direct observation
and evaluation at their points of impact with the managerial
decision domain. The four categories are (a) payments and
services by the government to the firm; (b) remission of
charges; (c) nonquantifiable, risk-reducing subsidies, and
(d) export subsidies. Although the fourth category (export
subsidies) includes elements of the other three categories, it
is nevertheless classified separately because subsidies in this
category are usually applied as separate entities, and when
adopting export subsidies governments often exhibit interests
extending far beyond those of the individual firm.

Each of the four categories listed above contains many
subsidies affecting industrial management, and these subsidies
will be dealt with under each individual heading.

PAYMENTS AND SERVICES BY THE GOVERNMENT
TO THE FIRM

Cash Grants

Cash grants usually are given as an incentive for investment either in a particular development region or for the development of a particular product or industry which the government is trying to advance. The size of this grant is usually a
function of the total investment required, or in proportion to
the investors' share in the proposed enterprise. For example,
Israel has two priority development regions, A and B, region
A having the higher priority. Consequently, the grant proportion allocated to firms willing to locate in region A is designed
to show a significant advantage as demonstrated in Table 2.

TABLE 2

Rate of Grant as Percentage of Total
Investment in Fixed Assets, Israel

	PRIORITY AREA A	PRIORITY AREA B	ALL OTHER AREAS
Building and Site Development	20%	15%	10%
Machinery and Equipment	33-1/3%	25%	20%

Source: Israel, State of Israel Investment Authority,
Government Incentives (Jerusalem, 1967), p. 3.

Tax Refunds

Since a tax refund subsidy may combine both direct cash
payments and remission of charges and is most commonly
used as an incentive for the manufacture of products for export, a more detailed discussion will follow when export subsidies will be dealt with. Tax refunds usually involve a return
of money by the government to the exporter, when the exporter
meets certain export criteria established by the government.

Loans at Reduced Interest Rates

As with cash grants the government may offer the prospective investor loans at interest rates significantly below the interest rates charged by banks and surely lower than the interest
rates charged on the black market. Again, the size of these
loans will be related to the total investment capital and will
vary both in size and interest rate, according to the importance
of the development region or the project. Table 3 demonstrates
the more favorable loans and interest rates given for development in regions A and B as compared with the rest of the
country.

TABLE 3

Loans and Interest Rates

	A AREA	B AREA	C AREA
Loan as Percent of Fixed Assets	55	50	45
Total of Grant and Loan as Percent of Fixed Assets	80	70	60
Interest Rate (percent)	6-1/2	8	10

Source: Israel, State of Israel Investment Authority,
Government Incentives (Jerusalem, 1967), p. 4.

Participation in Work-Force Training

In many countries the government will train or pay part
of the costs of training workers in order to bring them up to
the semiskilled level. The Israeli Ministry of Labor, for
example, will pay between IL250 and IL1,000* per worker for
on-the-job training. The Ministry will also pay part of the
costs of training workers who already have a trade but who
are trying to add to their abilities.[1]

---

*The official rate of exchange is $1 = IL3.50.

Subsidy for the Acquisition of Industrial Land
and Buildings

In some cases the government may provide free land; in other cases it may sell or lease land at very low prices. The government may also build the desired building and rent it to the investor, again at a low rent. In Israel, for example, standard buildings are leased at IL15 to IL18 per square meter per annum according to priority area. Nonstandard buildings will be constructed according to the investor's own specifications, and rented to him at 10 percent to 12 percent of the construction costs. The investor then retains the option to purchase the building within three years. Should the investor wish to construct the building himself, he can receive a 10-year loan of 50 percent of the building costs and a 50-month loan of 30 percent. In priority region A these loans are granted at 6.5 percent interest, while in region B the interest rate is 8 percent. [2] In the Netherlands, for example, if the ground area of the projected building takes up one-fifth or more of the site needed for location, the purchase price of the land will be reduced by 50 percent. Otherwise, the reduction is according to a sliding scale. Within two years, a further reduction may be allowed for the purchase of additional land for expansion purposes. The total reduction is limited to f 1,500,000. [*] In addition, a subsidy towards the building costs is given for a new factory building on an approved industrial site in a priority development region. These subsidies are given in the following amounts: f 30 per m^2 for the first 2,000 m^2 floor space, f 45 per m^2 for the second 2,000 m^2 floor space, and f 60 per m^2 for the excess over 4,000 m^2 floor space. In the lower priority development regions, the subsidy amounts to f 30 per m^2 for any floor space. The total subsidy in this category is limited to f 1,500,000. Within two years after delivery of the first subsidized building, an additional subsidy of f 30 per m^2 and up to f 300,000 may be obtained for expansion purposes. An alternative subsidy to all the above incentives is granted by the Dutch government in the form of 25 percent of the investment in land, buildings, and machinery, the maximum being f 3 million. [3]

In the United Kingdom the law specifies that:

Where machinery or plant qualifies for a grant, the amount will be 20 percent of the capital

---

[*]One guilder (f) = 27.62 cents.

expenditure concerned, unless it is "development area expenditure," in which case it will be 40 percent.[4]

Loans for Working Capital

In addition to the various subsidies already granted for the establishment of a company, special loans for working capital may be obtained. In Israel an investor locating in development region A is entitled to a loan of up to 50 percent of the total working capital needed at 9 percent interest per annum. The only restriction is that at least 20 percent of the necessary working capital must be financed out of the owner's capital. In region B the size of the loan is up to 40 percent, also at 9 percent interest per annum, with at least 30 percent of the working capital financed by the investor. In addition the government will finance all working capital for export, at 6 percent interest rate per annum, regardless of location.[5]

Transfer of Equipment

Should a company desire to transfer its facilities to development areas, it will receive grants to cover at least part, if not all, of the costs of transfer and the installation of equipment. In Israel this subsidy may amount to as much as IL1,000 per worker in region A and up to IL500 per worker in region B.[6]

Research Expenditures

Governments will always participate in financing industrial research. In Israel it is done on a fifty-fifty basis.[7] In Great Britain the costs of the plant and equipment used for research fall within the category of capital expenditures qualified for a grant and as such, the amount of the grant will be 40 percent of the expense in a development region, and 30 percent otherwise.[8]

Investment Survey

To encourage foreign investment some governments will bear either totally or partially the costs of on-the-spot investigations of prospective investment opportunities. The assumption is that an investor would like to make his own assessments prior to committing himself on the basis of government investment authority information. In Korea, for example, the Agency for International Development will assume 50 percent of the costs involved in making investment surveys. [9]

Subsidy Toward Interest Cost

A subsidy to help meet interest costs is given to an investor to help him meet his interest obligations including those that are accruing from government loans. In the Netherlands such a subsidy is given for a period of up to 15 years for a maximum of 3 percent per annum of the medium- and long-term loans used. [10]

Deferment of Fees

In addition to grants and loans, most fees usually associated with the establishment of a new enterprise are deferred to a future time (usually for five years). Fees in this category are, for instance, the registration fee and land transfer fee.

REMISSION OF CHARGES

Income Tax

Approved enterprises--those locating in high priority development regions or those manufacturing products which the government is trying to foster--are exempt from income tax and usually pay a smaller percentage of Company Profit Tax during the first couple of years.

In Israel, for example, the tax holiday lasts five years and the Company Profit Tax is set at 28 percent, commencing with the first year in which there is a chargeable income. [11]

Property Taxes

In Korea full exemption is allowed for corporation tax, property tax, and property acquisition tax for a period of five

years, and a 50 percent exemption is granted for the next
three years. [12]

In Israel only two-thirds of the property tax is exempt
during the first five years. [13]

Indirect Taxes and Charges

Approved enterprises are usually exempt from applicable
customs duty, purchase tax, and other indirect charges on
building materials and investment goods required for the establishment of the enterprise. These goods may be imported if
not locally produced, or if locally produced goods are not
competitive with the foreign product in price, quality, or delivery time. [14] In Korea customs duty and commodity tax on
imported installation equipment and raw materials are exempt
for a period of six months following the completion of construction. [15]

Investment in Securities

Investment in securities is an incentive intended for the
prospective foreign investor who cannot maintain constant
contact with the management of a locally established enterprise
or property, but who nevertheless may consider investment
under given conditions. To create such conditions the following
incentives are common:

1. Complete tax exemption on income from shares and
debentures negotiable through the local stock exchange provided (a) these investors do not enjoy double taxation relief
in their countries of residence with respect to such income,
and (b) they are residents of countries which have concluded
double taxation agreements with the country in which the investment is made. [16]

2. Complete exemption from Capital Gains Tax. [17]

Carry Forward Losses

In some countries losses are allowed to be carried forward
for a number of years. They can be deducted from income of
the same business, profession, or vocation in subsequent years.

If there is a loss in any one year, both the loss and depreciation
can be carried forward before depreciation allowances are
charged. Usually losses are carried forward for a limited
number of years, and depreciation sometimes for an indefinite
period. In Pakistan, for example, losses can be carried forward for six years. [18]

Immigrant Investors

Immigrant investors are usually exempt, partially or
totally, from income tax on all income derived abroad, for a
given period of time, usually five to seven years. In Israel
the individual investor is exempt for seven years. [19]

Accelerated Depreciation

Almost all depreciation policies are intended to allow
faster depreciation in the early years of the enterprise. Some
countries such as the Netherlands will accept, in principle,
any depreciation system, as long as it is based on the original
amount invested in the asset (replacement value not being accepted), and is applied with consistency. [20] Other countries
may actually specify the rate of depreciation which is allowed.
In Israel, for example, an approved enterprise is entitled to
a depreciation allowance of twice the usual rate for the first
five years of its use of plant, equipment, and machinery. In
cases of unusual wear and tear, a depreciation allowance of
two and a half times the usual rate may be granted, the usual
rates varying 7 percent to 20 percent per year for equipment
and machinery, 1 1/2 percent to 6 1/2 percent per year for
buildings, and 3 percent to 13 percent per year for buildings
housing equipment. [21]

In Pakistan, for example, the following depreciation allowances are stipulated:

1.   Initial depreciation, which is in addition to the normal
depreciation, is 25 percent on plant and installed machinery,
but machinery must not have been previously used in Pakistan.

2.   Initial depreciation at 15 percent is allowed on com-
mercial and industrial buildings, other than residential buildings for the labor force constructed between April 1, 1946, and
June 30, 1965.

3.   In the case of residential buildings for industrial labor constructed between April 1, 1954, and June 30, 1965 (both dates inclusive), initial depreciation at 25 percent of the cost thereof is allowed to the assessee.

4.   Double the normal rates of depreciation is allowed for a period of five years on plant and machinery installed on or after April 1, 1948, and before June 30, 1962.

5.   An extra allowance is given at 50 percent of the normal rates for double-shift working and at 100 percent of the normal rates for triple-shift working. [22]

All these incentives are in addition to the reminder that very liberal depreciation allowances are admissible in the early years of the establishment of an industrial undertaking.

Interest on Approved Loans

Interest payable on approved loans (approved region or approved industry) is sometimes fully exempt from tax, as in the case in Pakistan. [23]

Export Processing Zone

1.   Export zones are similar but not identical to free ports. Enterprises that are located in these zones must meet certain conditions, as, for example, in Taiwan: (a) that they are established with new investments; (b) that the establishment and operation of such enterprises will not adversely affect the operation of existing domestic industries also engaged in export; (c) that raw materials, semifinished, or finished products of such enterprises can be easily inspected or regulated; and (d) that the operation of such enterprises during the course of manufacture or production will not endanger public safety or public health inside the export processing zones.

2.   Enterprises that export goods want to be in an export processing zone because of additional tax benefits: (a) Machinery and equipment, raw materials, and semifinished products imported by export enterprises for their own use are exempt from import duties and dues. (b) All goods produced and all raw materials and semifinished products used by export

enterprises located in an export processing zone are exempt
from the commodity tax.

An example of an export processing zone is the Kaoshiung
Export Processing Zone (KEPZ) in Taiwan. [24] Free ports,
though somewhat different from export zones, could, under
certain conditions, be considered an incentive or subsidy.

NONQUANTIFIABLE, RISK-REDUCING SUBSIDIES

Subsidies Directly Affecting Management Decision

Loan Guarantees

The government may serve as a guarantor for a loan taken
by the investor in addition to the low-interest loans given to
him directly by the government. Such a guarantee assures
the creditor that the government will assume full responsibility
in repaying the loan should the borrower fail to do so. As
suggested by Professor C. Shoup, although the government
may never have to implement or carry out such an obligation,
it has nevertheless granted the borrower a subsidy equivalent
to the amount the public would be willing to pay, so as to be
relieved of such an obligation. [25] For example, the Republic
of China (Taiwan) has an investment guarantee agreement with
the United States. [26]

Government Guarantees of Foreign Investment

In order to minimize and reduce the persistent fear and
suspicion that foreign-owned businesses and property may be
nationalized or expropriated in future times, resulting in
losses to the investor who has to recoup his investment plus
the desired profit, a government will provide guarantees
against such occurrences. In Taiwan there is a 20-year
guarantee against expropriation if foreign ownership is 51 percent or more, and reasonable compensation for expropriation
of business with less foreign ownership. [27]

Right of Repatriation

The principal and profits derived from approved investments can be repatriated in the currency in which the investment was made. Usually, the entire amount may be withdrawn

at one time after a certain number of years if the investment
is realized. Otherwise, it may be withdrawn in equal yearly
sums as agreed upon with the proper authorities. In addition
a nonresident investor may transfer all or part of his investment to another nonresident against foreign currency, and
the transferee will receive all the benefits of a foreign currency investment for the unexpired period. In Israel this
period is five years. [28]

Repayment of Foreign Loans

A nonresident, who made an approved loan in foreign currency, may withdraw payments of principal and interest in
foreign currency. Sometimes accelerated repayment is per-
mitted if so desired. [29]

Transfer of Approved Loan

In Israel, for example, a nonresident who has received
Israeli currency as payment for his rights in an approved loan
may be entitled (a) to invest or lend all or part of the proceeds
in another project in Israel and retain the foreign currency
benefits or (b) to withdraw (from Israel) in foreign currency
all or part of the amount received, provided the amount withdrawn does not exceed the initial loan, plus interest less such
part of the loan as has already been paid. [30]

Availability of Research

Various research institutions, either sponsored by or
aided by governments, make their research facilities and
their advice available to industry. Some of these institutions
have as their main goal a given objective, such as the increase
of labor productivity, and may, consequently, be involved in
helping both new and established enterprises through training
courses. These training courses may be for anyone, from
laborers, to foremen, to senior management. Sometimes
these various services, research, consulting, and training
may be offered gratis or at low cost, since the government
most often will participate in financing such enterprises. [31]
In Taiwan the China Productivity and Trade Center (CPTC)
offers assistance in production problems, such as materials
handling, plant layout, work simplification, maintenance,
quality control, job evaluation, marketing, and in various
types of training problems. [32]

Regulation of Labor Disputes

Most governments, especially those in developing nations, know quite well that low wages are not necessarily enough of an inducement to attract foreign investment. Therefore, they try to stress the advantages of labor stability and pass various mandatory arbitration laws that will ensure management of at least a fair settlement in any future labor dispute. For example, in Taiwan, the Labor Dispute Arbitration Law stipulates that all disputes between workers and employers should be equitably arbitrated by special committees, and that workers should not resort to the suspension of businesses or the closing down of factories. In other words, strikes are not allowed. [33] Although such regulations may be common in many countries, nations that seek foreign investments reduce the risk of work stoppages and the loss of production by such regulations and other labor laws, thereby providing incentives to foreign investors.

Guaranteed Market

When a government is interested in establishing a manufacturing enterprise to produce a product for local consumption, and possibly for future export, it may sometimes promise or assure the investor of buying a certain quantity. Consequently, at least on one major consumer--the government--a monopoly is given to the manufacturer. This procedure is especially true with products of special interest to the military establishment, and explains why some small nations may be able to attract manufacturers of all sorts of military equipment. India, Israel, and the U. A. R. are examples of the many nations employing such an incentive.

Subsidies Indirectly Affecting Management Decision

Low Wages

The existence of a low level of wages is not necessarily the result of a country's need to industrialize and attract investments, but usually the result of historical socioeconomic factors. Nevertheless, the maintenance of relatively low wages through various government control or guidance methods can still be considered as an indirect subsidy to a foreign investor. (The size of the subsidy in this case will be the

difference between the labor costs in the low-wage region or
state and the higher labor costs in the next best alternative
location.) Thus, Taiwan, Korea and other developing nations
stress the low wages paid to unskilled and semiskilled labor,
while Israel stresses the low salaries of skilled technicians
and professionals. [34]

Special Conditions for Manpower

To minimize the acute problem of manpower availability,
be it unskilled, semiskilled, skilled, or professional, in the
development regions, various incentives are granted to persons
willing to join enterprises in such areas. In addition to somewhat higher wages than in the rest of the country (the differences
sometimes being subsidized by the government), personal income taxes in such regions are usually lower, thus providing
a nonquantifiable, indirect subsidy to industry locating in these
areas. (Israel has for many years had such a policy for
workers in the Negev, and especially in the port of Elath.)
Likewise at the professional level, approved specialists who
are also nonresidents are given such concessions for a limited
period of time. In Israel an approved specialist should pay no
more than 25 percent income tax for a period of three years. [35]
Regulations for continuing such practices for longer periods
are fairly flexible.

Product Protection

Many governments have set up special incentives for industries they wish to develop. In Israel examples of such industries are furs and leather goods (mainly fashion wear);
irrigation equipment; food processing equipment; equipment
for the chemical industry; medical and hospital equipment;
medical electronic equipment; prosthetics and equipment for
the physically disabled; electrical equipment; and industrial
diamond tools. The incentives may be in the form of the subsidies described so far or may take the form of tariffs intended
to protect the local market. These examples above were
drawn from a preliminary list of "preference" branches of
industry in which the government of Israel was particularly
interested in encouraging investments, in view of their promis-
ing export potential. The list was made public by the State of
Israel Investment Authority in December, 1966.

It is quite obvious that protecting a given industry, by
granting it a monopoly on the local market, can be considered

a subsidy. But the problem becomes more complex when one tries to consider tariffs and other various taxes on product substitutes. For example, to what extent can a luxury tax on imported television sets be considered a subsidy to the local manufacturers of radio sets? Or, can a special tax imposed on pipe tobacco be considered a subsidy to cigarette manufacturers? To answer these questions one would have to consider each product and its substitutes individually, and especially the degree to which it can be substituted. It is not within the scope of this book to carry out such an analysis but merely to point out that positive or negative incentives imposed on one product may be considered as a subsidy to another product.

The problem of tariffs is a sensitive one in a political sense, for governments will try to disguise their various protection methods in order not to influence their trade relations with other nations exporting products or substitutes. In this respect there is practically no nation that does not practice some sort of protective measures for its industry. It seems that free trade between nations is still a fairly distant dream, even though regional attempts such as the European Economic Market are being made.

Exchange Rate

Just as the maintenance of low wages can be considered an indirect subsidy to the manufacturer, so can the establishment of various exchange rates be considered, especially when exports or imports of raw materials, parts, equipment, or capital are involved. Governments may offer a lower or higher exchange rate for the import of needed equipment to promote the export of certain products, and the difference between these rates and the established rate can be construed as a subsidy. Similarly a devaluation of the local currency with respect to an international monetary standard--dollars, will have a subsidy-like effect on local exporters and on investments attached to the international standard.

EXPORT SUBSIDIES

The types of subsidies listed so far mainly were intended to promote investment in general and the development of certain priority regions and/or products in particular. However,

once the investment has been made, the company has been
established, and the production begins to flow, governments
may soon find out that the local market is too limited and does
not fit the economic scale of a viable enterprise. Coupled
with this realization is the necessity of having to balance trade
and produce hard currency available for purchases abroad.
The government, then, will attempt to persuade the manufacturers to export. Such a situation creates difficulties. Some
of the enterprises destined for export can hardly justify their
existence on the local market.

Originally, the government created artificial conditions
through the various types of subsidies for the establishment
of the enterprise. Now, in order to make these companies
export their products and compete on the world market, a
more concrete inducement must be found. The logical answer
is more subsidies--only this time the subsidies must be related somehow to export.

The use of export subsidies is common practice in practically every nation, especially developing nations trying to
promote export. Since the techniques do not vary much from
country to country we will concentrate on the official export
subsidies of just one country, namely, Israel.

The following list of export incentives is drawn directly
from the Israel Investors' Manual.[36]

Indirect Tax Refund

Indirect tax refunds are a means of compensating the exporter for indirect local taxes. The refund is granted on a
standard basis, in proportion to the added value of the exported
product in each branch. The rates of refund are given in
Table 4.

The refund is paid automatically, according to the invoice
accompanying each shipment abroad.

Refund of Taxes on Raw Materials
and Intermediate Products

Tax refunds on raw materials and intermediate products
are given to exporters regardless of whether the acquisition
is made locally or abroad. The refund usually includes custom
duties, purchase taxes, and other fees. In addition, similar
refunds are made on spare parts, components, accessory

TABLE 4

Export Incentives in Israel--Rates of Refund

PERCENT OF ADDED VALUE	RATE OF REFUND IN ISRAELI POUNDS FOR EACH DOLLAR EXPORT FOB
0-25	--
26-45	0.10
46-65	0.20
66 and Above	0.35

Source: Israel, State of Israel Investment Authority, Israel Investors' Manual (Jerusalem, 1968), p. 49.

equipment, and accessory materials. On these last items, the refund is not total but rather a function of the percentage of the yearly plant output which is exported.

Refund of Dock Fees on Imports for Reexport

Where direct import costs are more than 20 percent and where the FOB value of the exported value is larger than $330 per ton, dock fees are refunded.

Property Tax Refund on Equipment and Stock

Should a company export at least 27 percent of its yearly sales or at least 30 percent of its yearly production, it will be entitled to a property tax refund that year. The size of this refund will be related to the percentage export.

Travel Tax Exemptions for Approved Exporters

If a company has exported more than $100,000 in the previous year, its owners or employees will be exempt from travel taxes abroad. The number of exemptions are again related to the total value of export. It is assumed that these trips will benefit the company in such areas as promotion, marketing, and/or technical know-how.

Financing Export

Funds are established both in local and foreign currencies to grant credit to exporters at 6 percent yearly interest. Following are examples of the purpose of these funds.

Import Raw Materials for Production

In this case credit is granted for 180 days at 6 percent interest per annum (foreign currency).

Pay Production Costs

An Israeli plant that produces for export may receive credit in Israeli pounds to finance production costs at a rate of 80 percent of added value, until the product is shipped abroad. For each dollar added to the value of the product, IL2.80 is granted.

Export Shipments

When the goods are shipped additional credit is granted in Israeli pounds at a rate of 90 percent of the value of each shipment for a period of not more than six months.

Pay Purchase Taxes and Custom Duties

These payments may be deferred for nine months against a bank guarantee or other similar security.

Transport Services and Insurance

To encourage both importers and exporters to use the port of Elath, the government grants a refund. This refund usually is calculated as the difference between the cost of shipping or receiving products from the port of Haifa and the same cost from the port of Elath. The upper limit of this grant is 5 percent of the FOB value of the exports or imports. In addition a grant of up to 5 percent of the FOB value of exports will be granted for transhipment costs to countries to which Israel does not have direct transport lines, or where sailings are infrequent.

TABLE 5

Budgetary Industrial Export Subsidies, by Item, 1964-66
(Thousands of Israeli Pounds)

	1964	1965	1966
Refund of Taxes and Imposts			
Refund of Customs Duty on Accessories, Spare Parts, and Auxiliary Materials	166	362	1,147
Refund of War Risk Insurance (Arnona)	1,166	2,603	2,749
Refund of Taxes on Imports for Export Production (Property Tax on Stocks)	150	1,203	762
Refund of Travel Tax to Approved Exporters	116	250	100
Total	1,598	4,418	4,758
Direct Incentives			
Refund of Taxes on Imported Materials not Included in Special Arrangements	--	--	8,962
Refund of and Participation in Outlays			
Refund of Wharfage Fees on Imports for Export Production	920	1,499	2,937
Refund of Wharfage Fees on Exports	185	540	2,400
Participation in Goods Transport via Eilat	1,548	2,103	1,837
Foreign Trade Risk Insurance	69	799	734
Guarantee of Shipping Routes	4,739	1,904	1,535
Participation in Costs of Advertising, Market Research, and Maintenance of Sales Offices Abroad	1,383	2,031	3,173
Development and Research	229	1,307	6,907
Transshipment of Goods	124	473	793
Miscellaneous	1,756	887	45
Total	10,953	11,532	20,361
Subsidies to Export Companies			
Grant Based on Turnover of Export Companies	408	695	711
For Covering Losses of Export Companies	808	247	460
Total	1,216	942	1,171
Subsidies on Textile Products			
Participation in the Wool and Synthetic Products Fund	425	--	400
Grant for Exports of Garments from Imported Cloth	1,324	1,417	2,268
Subsidy on Yarn Exports	--	--	1,793
Subsidy on Cloth and Garment Exports	--	--	9,933
Refunds Because of Higher Raw Cotton Costs	--	--	934
Participation in Cotton Fund	500	3,967	4,189
Total	2,159	5,384	19,517
Grand Total	16,776	22,276	54,769

Source: Israel, Bank of Israel Annual Report 1966 (Jerusalem, May, 1967), p. 65.

Other Common Incentives Both Quantifiable
and Nonquantifiable

1. Foreign trade risk insurance covering 85 percent of
losses incurred.
2. Loans for advertising and market research at 6 percent to 7 percent for a period of 22 months.
3. Market research and promotional services through
various government institutes such as the Israel Export Institute and The Israel Company for Fairs and Exhibitions, LTD.
4. Assistance to export companies. Such companies,
organized according to industrial branch or area of export,
may receive grants amounting to .25 percent to 1.25 percent
of the FOB should this value exceed $250,000.

These are the types of export subsidies practiced in Israel.
Other countries may use some of these methods or may employ numerous variations of the same methods. In any case,
the underlying principle and usually the basic objective--the
encouragement of exports--will be the same; whether this
objective is achieved is another matter for discussion. Table
5 shows examples of export subsidies in Israel for 1964-66
and illustrates both the variety and the growing magnitude of
such subsidies. Table 6 compares the export subsidies in
Table 5 to the total industrial export for the comparable years.

TABLE 6

Total Industrial Export Versus
Industrial Export Subsidies
(millions of dollars)

	1964	1965	1966
Industrial Exports[1]	280.0	314.0	373.0
Industrial Export Subsidies[2]	5.6	7.4	18.2
Subsidies as a Percent of Total Industrial Export	2.0	2.4	4.9

[1]Israel, Ministry of Foreign Affairs, Information Division,
Facts About Israel 1969 (Jerusalem, 1970), p. 105.
[2]From Table 5.

TABLE 7

Examples of Subsidy Systems by Country

SUBSIDY SYSTEM	BRAZIL	BRITAIN[1]	CHINA (TAIWAN)	INDIA	IRELAND	ISRAEL	JAPAN[2]
Payments and Services by the Government to the Firm							
Cash Grants			x			x	
Tax Refunds					x	x	
Loans at Reduced Interest Rates			x		x	x	
Participation in Work Force Training	x		x			x	
Subsidy Towards Acquisition of Land, Buildings			x	x	x	x	
Loans for Working Capital						x	
Aid in Equipment Transfer						x	
Research Expenditures			x			x	
Investment Survey				x		x	
Subsidy Towards Interest Payments						x	
Deferment of Fees						x	
Remission of Charges							
Income Tax	x		x	x	x	x	
Property Taxes	x		x	x		x	
Indirect Taxes and Charges	x		x		x	x	
Investment in Securities						x	
Carry Forward Losses			x		x	x	
Immigrant Investors						x	
Accelerated Depreciation	x	x	x		x	x	
Interest on Approved Loans--Tax						x	
Export Processing Zone			x			x[3]	
Nonquantifiable, Risk-Reducing Subsidies							
Loan Guarantees						x	
Government Guarantees of Foreign Investment	x		x	x		x	x
Right of Repatriation	x		x	x		x	x
Repayment of Foreign Loans	x		x			x	
Transfer of Approved Loan						x	
Research and Consulting Institutions	x		x	x		x	x
Regulation of Labor Disputes	x		x			x	
Guaranteed Market					x	x	x
Low Level of Wages			x	x		x	x
Special Conditions for Manpower						x	
Product Protection	x	x	x	x	x	x	x
Exchange Rate						x	
Export Subsidies							
Export Subsidy-Tax Refund						x	
Refund of Dock Fees						x	
Refund of Property Tax on Equipment (Export)						x	
Travel Tax Exemptions						x	
Financing Export			x			x	
Transport Services and Insurance						x	
Foreign Trade Risk Insurance			x		x	x	
Loans for Advertising and Market Research						x	
Promotional Services and Assistance to Export Company			x	x	x	x	x

22

	COUNTRY						
SUBSIDY SYSTEM	KOREA	MEXICO	NETHER-LANDS	PAKISTAN	PERU	SPAIN	USA[4]
Payments and Services by the Government to the Firm							
Cash Grants							x
Tax Refunds	x						x
Loans at Reduced Interest Rates	x		x	x	x	x	x
Participation in Work Force Training	x	x	x		x		
Subsidy Towards Acquisition of Land, Buildings	x	x	x	x	x	x	x
Loans for Working Capital							
Aid in Equipment Transfer							
Research Expenditures						x	x
Investment Survey	x						
Subsidy Towards Interest Payments			x				
Deferment of Fees							
Remission of Charges							
Income Tax	x	x		x	x	x	x
Property Taxes	x	x		x	x	x	x
Indirect Taxes and Charges	x	x	x	x	x	x	x
Investment in Securities						x	
Carry Forward Losses		x	x	x			
Immigrant Investors							
Accelerated Depreciation	x	x	x	x	x	x	
Interest on Approved Loans--Tax					x		
Export Processing Zone				x			
Nonquantifiable, Risk-Reducing Subsidies							
Loan Guarantees							x
Government Guarantees of Foreign Investment	x	x		x	x	x	
Right of Repatriation	x	x	x	x	x	x	
Repayment of Foreign Loans	x	x			x	x	
Transfer of Approved Loan							
Research and Consulting Institutions	x		x	x			
Regulation of Labor Disputes	x		x		x		
Guaranteed Market							
Low Level of Wages	x	x		x	x		x
Special Conditions for Manpower					x		
Product Protection	x	x		x	x	x	x
Exchange Rate							
Export Subsidies							
Export Subsidy-Tax Refund	x						
Refund of Dock Fees							
Refund of Property Tax on Equipment (Export)	x	x	x	x			
Travel Tax Exemptions							
Financing Export					x		
Transport Services and Insurance					x		x
Foreign Trade Risk Insurance							
Loans for Advertising and Market Research							x
Promotional Services and Assistance to Export Company	x	x	x	x		x	x

[1]Britain moved in 1966 from a system of investment allowances mainly through tax incentives to investment grants.

[2]Japan until recently refrained from encouraging foreign investments; hence, their direct subsidies to foreigners are insignificant, the main contribution being low-wage system.

[3]Israeli Free Port in planning stage.

[4]The predominant subsidies in the United States on the federal level are industry-wide subsidies (shipping, oil), and until present the 7 percent tax credit which the present administration is seeking to drop. On the other hand, states have employed practically every subsidy system used by foreign countries.

Source: Drawn from the various publications listed in the Bibliography.

A relatively high percentage of export subsidies was needed to generate additional industrial exports, thereby offsetting to some extent the benefits derived from the growth in exports. The list of subsidies described thus far can be summarized by Table 7, which is by no means conclusive. Although several countries appear not to employ some of the incentives listed, this may not be the case in reality. Some countries tend to generalize in their subsidy definitions, leaving details for individual arrangement. Only in the case of Israel, Korea, and Pakistan is there a fairly clear-cut definition of each subsidy system as outlined by the relevant authorities.

NOTES

1. State of Israel Investment Authority, Israel Investors' Manual (Jerusalem, 1968), p. 67.

2. Ibid., p. 46.

3. Amsterdam-Rotterdam Bank, Commerce and Industry in the Netherlands: A Base for Business Operations in Europe (Amsterdam, 1967), pp. 45-46.

4. F. H. Brittenden, A Guide to Investment Grants (London: Butterworth, 1966), p. 4.

5. Israel Investors' Manual, op. cit., p. 47.

6. Ibid.

7. Ibid., p. 73.

8. Brittenden, op. cit., pp. 10-12.

9. Economic Planning Board, Office of Investment Promotion, Investment Guide to Korea (Seoul, 1967), p. 21.

10. Commerce and Industry in the Netherlands, op. cit., p. 46.

11. Israel Investors' Manual, op. cit., p. 19.

12. Investment Guide to Korea, op. cit., p. 19.

13. Israel Investors' Manual, op. cit., p. 19.

14. Ibid.

15. Investment Guide to Korea, op. cit., p. 18.

16. Israel Investors' Manual, op. cit., p. 23.

17. Ibid., p. 24.

18. Department of Investment Promotion and Supplies, Guide to Investment in Pakistan (Karachi: Government of Pakistan Press, 1964), p. 10.

19. Israel Investors' Manual, op. cit.

20. Commerce and Industry in the Netherlands, op. cit., p. 35.

21. Israel Investors' Manual, op. cit., p. 19.

22. Guide to Investment in Pakistan, op. cit., p. 9.

23. Ibid., p. 10.

24. Bank of America National Trust and Savings Association, Focus on Taiwan: An Economic Study of the Republic of China (New York, 1968), p. 16.

25. Carl S. Shoup, Public Finance (Chicago: Aldine, 1969), p. 149.

26. Focus on Taiwan, op. cit.

27. Ibid.

28. Israel Investors' Manual, op. cit., p. 20.

29. Ibid., p. 21.

30. Ibid.

31. Ibid., p. 69.

32. China Productivity and Trade Center, pamphlet (Taipei, October 31, 1967).

33. Industrial Development and Investment Center, A Brief Report on the Supply of Labor in Taiwan (Taipei, 1967), p. 6.

34. See Ibid. and also Israel Investors' Manual, op. cit., pp. 55-64.

35. Ibid., p. 23.

36. Ibid., pp. 49-53.

CHAPTER **2** THE FINANCIAL
DECISIONS

Generally, a firm faces three basic financial decisions:
(1) the area and size of the investment, (2) the source or
sources of its funds--or the capital structure of the firm, and
(3) the distribution of profits. [1] This chapter will observe the
impact of subsidy systems on the first two of these decisions,
for these decisions have a lasting effect on the operational
character of the firm.

As we noted earlier, a large portion of the subsidies listed
in the previous chapter influences the investment decision. As
suggested earlier, some governments, especially those of developing nations, seek to encourage investments to promote
the economy in general or to promote a given product, industry,
or region in particular. Should the rate of return on investments in developmental areas be higher than the return from
other alternative investment opportunities, a firm or individual
investor would rank such an investment high on the capital
expenditure schedule. Or, in other words, the normal rate
of return on such investments would be sufficient to draw a
desired level of investment. However, some of these investments, when tested by established engineering-economy
criteria, show a disadvantage in comparison to alternative
opportunities. Thus, the government must resort to subsidies
in order to make such investments seem feasible in the evaluation process. This governmental interference leads towards
a review of investment criteria and an examination of the influence of subsidies on these measurements.

Investments can be evaluated through a variety of methods.
This volume will not discuss the merits and deficiencies of
these methods, but merely will look at some of the more
common methods and try to evaluate the impact of subsidies
on these criteria of evaluation.

In industrial engineering the more common methods of
measuring proposed investments are the payback period, the
rate of return on the investment (or on additional investment),

annual cost, and present-worth comparisons. We shall observe
that the subsidies listed in Chapter 1 are designed to make a
seemingly inferior investment opportunity one that will become
desirable by accepted methods of evaluation.

PAYBACK PERIOD

This method of evaluation is especially useful in developing countries where political instability becomes a negative
factor in the considerations of a long-term investment project.
Those subsidies listed in Table 7 which belong to the first
category, namely, cash payments and services, allow a reduction in the investor's capital outlays for the project thereby
making it possible to recover the investment (exclusive of the
subsidy) in a shorter payback period. The subsidies belonging
in the second category influence the payback period criterion
from two different directions. The remissions of charges
permit higher after-tax profits, thus allowing a faster capital
recovery; and at the same time accelerated depreciation techniques legalize the early recovery of a major portion of the
investment and/or the shortening of the accounting life span of
this investment. Obviously, if the payback period is a crucial
yardstick for investment and if the subsidy is large enough to
alter the payback period for a given investment opportunity,
it is conceivable that management would choose the subsidized
alternative in lieu of a non-subsidized alternative showing a
longer payback period.

RATE OF RETURN ON INVESTMENT

For each capital investment opportunity one usually tries
to determine the prospective rate of return. This rate of return takes into consideration the risk and uncertainty involved
in each project. Should one desire to invest a certain sum it
is obvious that he should select projects that yield the highest
rate of return on the investment. If the government desires
to promote a specific product for manufacturing or a certain
geographical region for plant location, and if doing so means
accepting a lower rate of return by the firm, then the sum
total of subsidies and benefits offered by the government to the
firm should be larger or at least equal to the prospective losses
that the firm stands to incur.

Theoretically, one could develop a schedule showing the demand for investment funds according to a decreasing rate of return.[2] Such a demand schedule when plotted will look like Figure 1.

At a given rate of return r_1 the company is willing to invest I_1 dollars. The company will not invest I_2 dollars since the rate of return on the increment I_2-I_1 will be less than r_1 which is the desired rate of return established through company policy. As a matter of fact, the incremental investment I_2-I_1 yields a return which is less than the return desired by the shaded area ABC. To justify I_2-I_1, S should be greater than ABC. For example, the government may give a cash grant of I_3-I_2, thereby increasing the total investment in the project up to I_3. Usually the additional return on this subsidy, although at a rate $r_3 < r_2$, will be larger than the implied potential loss ABC (I_2I_3CD is greater than ABC). In many cases the receiver of the subsidy may utilize the subsidy cash grant or loan at a low interest rate for earnings at r_1, in which case his return on the subsidy I_3-I_2 is the area I_2I_3BE, a figure obviously larger than ABC. In case of a loan he will earn the difference between the rate at which the loan is given and the actual realized rate.

If the cash grants and loan interest rates create favorable conditions of investment, then it is conceivable that a project may show a lower rate of return on the additional investment than the desired rate, but a higher rate of return under the impact of subsidies.

ANNUAL COST COMPARISONS--
NET PRESENT VALUE

In the various annual cost comparisons, each alternative investment is evaluated with respect to the total yearly costs required. Under objective evaluation the rule is to select that alternative which produces the lowest annual costs. If a subsidy is granted on a year-to-year basis, then each year the subsidy will have to be at least equal to the difference between the annual costs of the subsidized project and the estimated annual costs of the best alternative. On the other hand if the subsidy is granted only once, then it has to be at least equal to the present value of the series of such yearly differences in costs. In this sense the annual comparison method is similar to the net present value method.

The net present value of the project is usually defined as

FIGURE 1

Schedule of Cumulative Demand for Capital

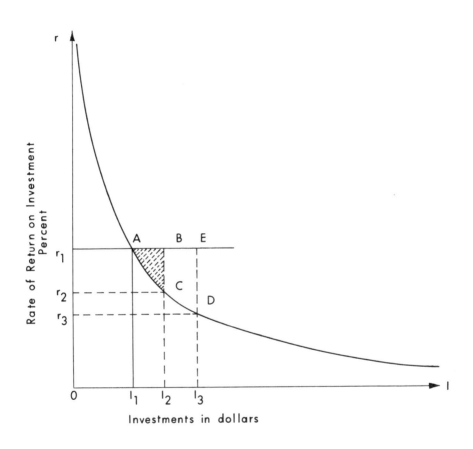

I = Investment funds that can be invested and which will earn at least the respective rate of return.

r = The expected rate of return on the investment.

S = Total government subsidy.

the present value of the cash inflows less the present value of the cash outflows.[3] To demonstrate the influence of subsidies on the application of this evaluation technique let us define the following

R_i = revenue in period i; i=1, . . ., n

C_i = costs incurred in period i

r = rate of return on the investment

I = required investment

n = life of investment

P = present value of a series of future profits due to the investment I at rate of return r.

NPV = net present value

The net revenue for each period is equal to $R_i - C_i$. Hence, the present value of all such future net revenues will be

$$P = (R_1 - C_1) \frac{1}{(1+r)} + (R_2 - C_2) \frac{1}{(1+r)^2} + \ldots + (R_n - C_n) \frac{1}{(1+r)^n}$$

$$P = \sum_{i=1}^{n} (R_i - C_i) \frac{1}{(1+r)^i}$$

Hence, the net present value is equal to

$$NPV = \sum_{i=1}^{n} (R_i - C_i) \frac{1}{(1+r)^i} - I$$

Obviously, when comparing various investment alternatives, the alternative with the highest present net value will be chosen. If investment I shows NPV_1 for Project 1 and NPV_2 for Project 2 where NPV_1 is greater than NPV_2, then should the government decide to subsidize Project 2 the present value of such subsidies must be larger than or equal to $NPV_1 - NPV_2$.

These last methods relate the total size subsidies to a series of future costs and revenues. But since future costs and revenues can only be estimated, one must make subsidies a function of the more pessimistic of the estimates. Such determination of subsidy size leads to inefficiency in the allocation of subsidies on the donor's side and, at the same time, it makes the governments' subsidy program susceptible to manipulations (such as cost overruns) by investors and firms seeking to maximize and perpetuate the inflow of subsidies.

The decision to invest in a project requiring a subsidy to become feasible directly affects the second of the financial decisions, the capital structure of the subsidized firm. The most significant impact that subsidies seem to have on this decision is the rather low ratio of equity capital to capital

obtained either through grants or various subsidized or
nonsubsidized loans. An analysis of Tables 9 and 10 and
Figure 3 demonstrates the decrease in the equity capital ratio
in Israel over the years. The definition of equity for the
Israeli data includes proprietary accounts. Had these accounts
been excluded, then the equity figure for 1956 and 1957 would
drop to 25 percent.[4] It is interesting to note (Table 10) that
the other country with a low equity ratio is India, which also
is included in the sample of subsidy-employing nations described in Chapter 1.

It is true that other factors, such as the existence of only
a limited stock market exchange and inflationary trends with
consequent monetary devaluations, contribute greatly to this
low ratio; but nevertheless, subsidy systems provide the
financial conditions that enable the maintenance of such low
equity ratios.

The availability of government grants and subsidized short-
and long-term loans enable the private investor to limit his own
financial involvement in the firm. Tables 8 and 9, and Figures
2 and 3 clearly indicate an inverse relationship between the
availability of grants and subsidies and equity capital. As the
sum of government grants and loans grew in size over the
years, equity capital tended to decrease. In other words the
expansion of government financial involvement in industrial
firms enabled the private investor to reduce his own financial
participation in the project.

As indicated in Chapter 1 each of the subsidy systems is
intended to achieve a given objective, to increase investment,
create employment, and so forth. But, due to the multiplicity
of factors considered in the management decision process, it
is very difficult to establish clearly whether the various incentives actually yield the desired results, and, if so, how
successfully. Apparent trends may or may not be attributed
to a specific incentive. An example of such an ambiguous
situation is the case of Israel. Tables 8, 9, and 10, and
Figures 2 and 3 indicate a possible impact of subsidy systems
on two major managerial decisions. One is the investment
decision whose process under the mechanics of the subsidy
system was described above.

Figure 2 indicates that such an impact occurred, especially
for 1967 when both government subsidies and investments rose
sharply. The Government Investment Authority officials like
to view this sharp increase as a direct response to an amendment to the investment law that was passed April 22, 1967, and
which further increased the incentives for investment.[5] While
this interpretation can and is being disputed, there seems to be

TABLE 8

Sources for Investment Capital in Manufacturing
Industries, Israel, 1960-67 ($1,000)

YEAR	TOTAL INVEST-MENT	GOVERN-MENT PARTICI-PATION	PRIVATE BANK LOANS	TOTAL NON-PRIVATE CAPITAL[1]	TOTAL PRIVATE INVEST-MENT (EQUITY TOTAL)[2]
1960	166,621	59,800	5,406	65,206	101,415
1961	304,011	58,608	12,209	70,817	233,094
1962	160,657	39,564	2,374	41,938	118,719
1963	180,449	52,623	6,227	58,850	121,599
1964	261,581	66,771	14,087	80,858	180,723
1965	222,252	70,979	7,371	78,350	143,902
1966	255,710	73,608	20,714	94,322	161,388
1967	676,093	322,268	49,048	371,326	304,767

[1] Column 4 is derived by adding Columns 2 and 3.
[2] Column 5 is derived by subtracting Column 4 from Column 1.

Source: State of Israel Investment Authority, Israel
Investment Authority Report for 1967 (Jerusalem, January,
1968), p. 7.

agreement as to the impact of subsidies on the other decision;
namely, the subsidized company's financial structure. It is
quite obvious that the increase in subsidies leads to an increase
in the overall proportion of non-equity capital, and from Figure
2 it is evident that in the case of Israel (in 1967) the total of
government grants and loans surpassed the total private investment, thus making the ratio of private to total investment
even lower.

This low private capital ratio creates the necessity for
short-term loans to finance operating expenditures, credit to
customers, and the return of investment loans. Consequently,
a vicious cycle is created. The government grants investment
loans at low interest rates. Unprofitable companies unable to
return these loans borrow at high interest rates to return the
original low interest loans. If one has to add some 10 percent

FIGURE 2

Total Investment in Manufacturing,
Government Loans and Grants to Investment in Manufacturing
1960-1967

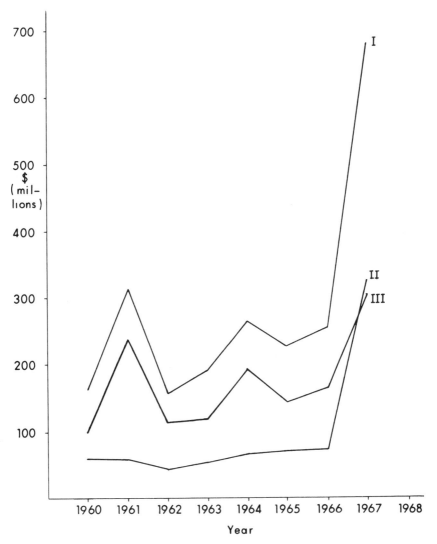

I: Total investment in manufacturing.
II: Government subsidies and loans.
III: Private Investment.

Source: Columns 1, 2, and 5 in Table 8.

TABLE 9

Non-Equity Capital and Government Grants
and Loans as a Percentage of Total
Investment, Israel, 1961-67

YEAR	NON-EQUITY CAPITAL AS A PERCENT OF INVESTMENT[1]	GOVERNMENT GRANTS AND LOANS AS A PERCENT OF TOTAL INVESTMENT[2]
1961	23.3	19.3
1962	26.1	24.7
1963	32.8	28.6
1964	31.0	25.6
1965	35.2	31.9
1966	37.0	28.8
1967	55.0	47.6

[1] Column 1 was derived from Table 8 by dividing Column 4 by Column 1.

[2] Column 2 was derived from Table 8 by dividing Column 2 by Column 1.

to the price of a finished product to cover high interest costs, while the competitors capital cost may be only at 5 percent, the high interest paying product will exhibit a definite cost disadvantage even if all other factors are equal.

But this high interest rate is only one of the important factors for the nonprofitability of some subsidized companies. In their search to avoid such unfortunate ventures, investors must look at other investment criteria, such as the degrees of risk and uncertainty associated with a given investment.

Usually risk and uncertainty are differentiated by associating risk with known probabilities of outcome, and uncertainty with either unknown or partially known probabilities. [6] The variety of subsidies that the government puts at the investor's disposal serves by itself as a risk-reducing factor in the investment considerations. Again some qualitative nonquantifiable systems are so designed as to influence and alter the decisions one would reach by employing these criteria. When a government promises a manufacturer that it will purchase a certain percentage of his output for a given number

FIGURE 3

Non-Equity Capital and Government Grants and Loans as a Percentage of Total Investment in Approved Manufacturing Enterprises in Israel, 1961-1967

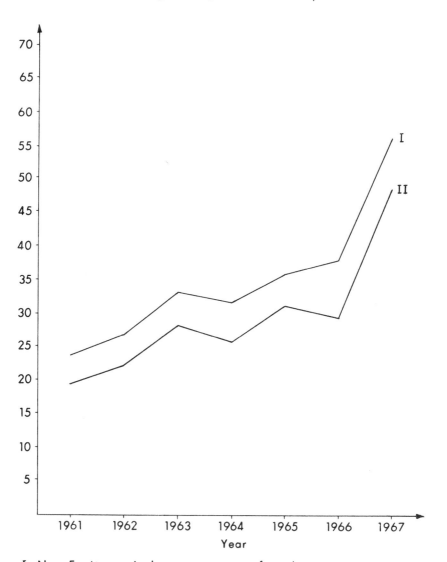

I: Non-Equity capital as percentage of total investment.
II: Government grants and loans as a percentage of total investments.

Source: Table 9.

TABLE 10

Ratio of Equity Capital to Total Balance
Sheet in Industrial Companies,
Israel and Other Countries

COUNTRY	YEAR	PERCENT
Israel	1950	51
	1954	41
	1955	35
	1956	39
	1957	38
	1958	37
United States of America	1958	64
Canada	1957	67
Great Britain	1958	60
Australia	1958	63
Colombia	1958	69
India	1958	37
Austria	1959	54
Sweden	1958	50
Denmark	1958	48

Sources: Bank of Israel, "The Financial Structure of
Israel's Industrial Companies," Bank of Israel Bulletin, 17
(Jerusalem, January, 1963), p. 61; "Changes in the Financial
Structure of Israel's Industrial Companies, 1956/57 to
1961/62," Bank of Israel Bulletin, 19 (Jerusalem, May, 1963),
p. 29.

of years, what was originally a decision under uncertainty
(in this case uncertainty of demand for his product) is changed
into a decision under certainty. Now all he has to do is decide
whether the venture is risky or not. Again, subsidies help
him reduce his doubts. When a person invests his own capital
in a project that may seem risky, he will think twice. But
when his investment is only a small portion of the total capital
invested, with the government a passive partner, he will not
mind taking greater risks. He knows quite well that the government in caring for its own share of the investment will come
to his rescue in times of trouble. In this case, even though he
will still be trying to maximize profits, he would not hesitate
to try some risky ventures for quick returns and some profits
at the expense of his partner.

Such ventures occur especially during the first years of
the enterprise when profits are either low or nonexistent. To
cite an extreme example in Israel it will be enough to quote
Minister Mordechai Bentov, appropos of Jimmy Levis' textile
company in Nazareth.

> So far there were speculators that were granted
> government loans at a nominal level of 80 percent,
> while in practice they received even 100 percent or
> 110 percent of their investment. Hence, people like
> Jimmy Levi were able to pocket some IL2 million,
> even before the first cornerstone was placed. [7]

This particular case became a cause célèbre in Israel
during the late 1950's. In its endeavors to create employment
in the city of Nazareth, the government helped finance Mr.
Levis' textile company with large loans which he was able to
draw and use for various purposes, while work toward the
accomplishment of the real goals proceeded at a rather slow
pace. After this incident, the Israeli government established
certain controls to ensure that such an event would not reoccur.
One such control was the requirement that investors commit
a portion of their own capital prior to drawing government
loans. Nevertheless, the number of undiscovered cases may
be numerous, and only a few of them are discovered at a stage
early enough to prevent sizeable losses. No country is really
immune to the above incidents. Wherever governments tend
to subsidize industry regardless of tight control, would-be
speculators will always find loopholes permitting them to take
advantage of the subsidy without involving their own capital
and often without even enhancing the purpose for which the
subsidy was granted.

Not only do subsidies become susceptible to speculative manipulations as in the example cited above, but indirectly they also cause other risky ventures, even after the individual investor has committed his own capital to the establishment of the firm. These risky ventures are made possible because of the low equity ratio resulting from the availability of government grants and loans. By accepting such grants and loans, an investor creates a partnership with the government, thereby reducing the risk to his own share of the capital invested. Once his capital is relatively safe (in some cases it may even be recovered), he may tend to gamble and enter ventures even more speculative, with the entire capital.

As suggested earlier, the resulting failure of many of these risky ventures becomes an unnecessary burden on the national economy. The government as the silent partner usually ends up taking a major proportion of losses suffered. It is difficult to assess the overall costs of this burden to the economy. We cannot know the costs of alternative investments made, or if all the subsidies channelled to other projects benefited the society in general rather than the few who were involved by having invested a small portion.

In Israel the economy paid partially for this inefficiency when during a two-year period of economic slowdown the government tried to eliminate all "parasite" industries. As Minister of Finance P. Sapir in his 1967-68 budget address noted,

> Inefficient enterprises will not be able to go on interminably and the price of the inevitable collapse will be paid not only by the owners--the workers, too, will be saddled with a large part of the burden. [8]

But as long as the subsidy system continues, inefficient companies whose viability is entirely dependent on subsidies will survive.

NOTES

1.   James T. S. Porterfield, Investment Decisions and Capital Costs (Englewood Cliffs, N. J.: Prentice-Hall, 1965), p. 5.

2.   Joel Dean, Managerial Economics (Englewood Cliffs, N. J.: Prentice-Hall, 1962), p. 561.

3. Porterfield, op. cit., p. 30.

4. Bank of Israel, "The Financial Structure of Israel's Industrial Companies," Bank of Israel Bulletin, 17 (Jerusalem, January, 1963), p. 37.

5. State of Israel Investment Authority, Law For the Encouragement of Capital Investment (Jerusalem, January, 1967), p. 8.

6. Norman N. Barish, Economic Analysis for Engineering and Managerial Decision-Making (New York: McGraw-Hill, 1962), p. 8.

7. M. Bentov, "Technology Determines the Output," Economic Quarterly, 53 (Tel Aviv, June, 1967), p. 41.

8. P. Sapir, The Three E's: Efficiency, Employment, Export, 1967/68 Budget Address, December 20, 1966 (Jerusalem: Government Press, 1967).

CHAPTER **3** THE LOCATION
DECISION

Once a firm has decided to invest it must then decide on
the location of its plant. As this location decision involves a
large investment in fixed assets especially in the building or
purchase of facilities, and may usually be considered an irreversible decision affecting both short- and long-term considerations of the company, the decision is one of major
proportions. In this chapter the possible effects of subsidy
programs on this decision including the selection process and
the site evaluation criteria will be investigated.

As suggested in Chapter 1, subsidy systems are designed
to generate investments from both domestic and foreign
sources. If the investment in a new enterprise is from local
sources, the location decision is a one-step decision involving
the analysis of alternative sites and the choice of the best alternative. On the other hand, should the investment be from
a foreign source, then the location decision becomes a two-
step decision. The first decision the foreign investor has to
make is "where in the world should we put that plant."[1] Only
then will he have to go through the phase common to the domestic investor, namely, the site selection.

Unless a company has a subjective interest in a given
country, the task of choosing the best foreign venture is
very complex. The vast number of alternatives "coupled
with the lack of adequate information, shortage of time, and
possible cost militate against extensive screening. So most
international investments are made out of fear that a market
may be lost, as a reaction to a deal offered by an outsider or
sometimes simply by hunch."[2] Barring hunches or special
deals there is a set of important variables that have to be
analyzed prior to choosing the country in which to invest.
These variables are usually divided into two major categories:
country-related variables and product-related variables. In
the first category are factors such as market size, investment climate, level of technology, wage rates, and distance

from competing industries. In the second category are distribution problems, economics of scale, and consumers' need
for the product. It is the purpose of subsidy systems to affect
some of these variables making them more attractive to investors.

Since a majority of the factors enumerated above do not
lend themselves to easy quantification, most subsidy systems
affecting these factors belong to the nonquantifiable class. The
usual method of evaluating nonquantifiable factors is by using
the point-system method. The underlying principle of this
method is assigning point values to each factor under a weighted
rating scale. Eventually, the alternative with the highest point
value will be accepted as the best choice.[3] Data for some of
the sample countries, China, Korea, and Israel,[4] indicates an
increase of foreign capital invested in these countries over the
past few years. The increase is attributed by the proponents
of subsidy programs to the introduction of these subsidies,
thereby creating conditions attractive to foreign investment.
On the other hand, opponents of subsidies tend to associate
such an increase in investments with the general growth of
the economy, and not specifically with the availability of subsidies. This particular contention is further strengthened by
the fact that it is the nonquantifiable class of subsidies that
comes closest to influencing the investment decision. A look
at both country-related and product-related variables mentioned earlier suggests that a variable under which subsidies
could be examined is the investment-climate variable. As
demonstrated in Chapter 1, the variety of risk-reducing subsidy programs that a country employs may improve its investment-climate image. But this particular variable seems
to be less important than such variables as market size,
availability of local technology, and distance from raw materials. In the case of Israel, for example, the present expansion of investments in the electronics industry is generally
attributed to defense requirements and to Israel's desire following the Six-Day War for self-sufficiency in arms production. In other words actual subsidies were not the primary
factor in the decision to develop the Israeli electronics industry. A similar example is the migration of American industrial companies to Mexico. At this time some two hundred United
States companies have moved across the southern border to
Mexico.[5] This movement has been facilitated by the Mexican
government's desire to develop the region close to the American border and create employment there. It permits American
companies to bring equipment into Mexico tax free and ex-
empts them from income taxes for a given number of years.

Despite these subsidies the migration of American companies
south of the Rio Grande is attributed mainly to low wages for
unskilled workers and to the lack of unionization. Companies
obviously take advantage of these subsidies, but had these
subsidies not been granted, the low wages and lack of unionization would have been sufficient inducements in the relocation
considerations. In the two examples above the dominant
criteria were a guaranteed market and low wages, factors
listed in the classification of nonquantifiable subsidies, which
usually do not involve an actual contribution by the government to the manufacturing enterprise. Such conditions generally are considered natural incentives and make these
countries more desirable than other countries for investment purposes. Therefore, the opponents of subsidy programs contend that investments would have been made in such
countries regardless of government subsidies. It is suggested
that in such cases subsidies serve merely as the "icing on the
cake." In view of these arguments and the fact that less
subsidy-oriented countries have also shown an increase in
investments consistent with their economic growth, one may
infer that the proof offered by some governments, that investments grew as a function of subsidies, is not decisive. In the
case of Israel, for example, manufacturing foreign currency
approvals show only small variations for the period 1963-66
(see Table 11 and Figure 4) despite existing subsidy programs.
Only in 1967 did Israel experience a sudden increase in foreign
investments in industry. Again there is no circumstantial
evidence that this sharp increase in investments is directly
related to the extension of the Law for the Encouragement of
Investments (April, 1967) and not to the overall economic
boom that characterized 1967.

It must be noted at this point that subsidies do affect the
decisions of certain investors; namely, the speculator, who
with limited resources at his disposal, seeks opportunities
for a high return on his investment within a short payback
period. The motivation of such an investor was discussed to
some extent at the end of Chapter 2. In reality this is a new
class of investors, most of whom are absentee owners rely-
ing on local management. Their main sphere of activity and
expertise lies in the optional manipulation of the various subsidy programs. Companies whose owners and managers fall
within this category cannot be judged by ordinary criteria.
Consequently, a separate chapter (Chapter 5) is devoted to a
description and analysis of this phenomenon.

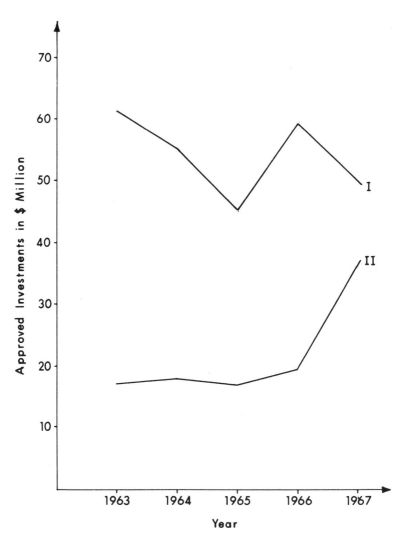

FIGURE 4

Approved Investments in Foreign Currency
Israel, 1963 –1967

I: Total foreign currency approvals.
II: Manufacturing foreign currency approvals.

Source: Table 11.

TABLE 11

Investment Approvals in Foreign Currency,
Israel, 1963-67

YEAR	MANUFACTURING FOREIGN CURRENCY APPROVALS	TOTAL FOREIGN CURRENCY APPROVALS IN $1,000
1963	16,896	61,557
1964	17,854	55,393
1965	16,878	45,751
1966	18,907	59,706
1967	36,766*	49,168

*Even though this rise is attributed by the Israeli Invest-
ment Authority to the introduction of grants according to
the April 12, 1967, amendment, it is still too early to judge
whether this attribution is valid. The political aspect of
1967 may have contributed more directly to the increase
in foreign investments than the grants themselves.

Source: State of Israel Investment Authority, Israel
Investment Authority Report for 1967 (Jerusalem, January,
1968), p. 6.

SITE SELECTION

When selecting the location of their plant, the aim of all
entrepreneurs is to find that site for which "the utility will be
as great as possible."[6] Whether they actually succeed in finding such an ideal location can only be determined at a later
date, and will depend upon the consideration they gave to
the various quantitative and nonquantitative location factors
and on the valuation techniques employed.

The many techniques developed and the various attempts
to incorporate a theory of plant location into the general
framework of economics have been largely German in origin.
Economists such as J. H. von Thünen, Alfred Weber, and
Tord Palander have made the most significant contributions in
this area.[7] Their techniques involve finding the lowest CIF
(cost, insurance, freight), by finding the point of minimum

transport cost through the construction of isodapanes (lines
of equal total freight per unit of product); and isovectures
(lines representing equal unit freight rates), the point of
lowest total cost, or the point of greatest profit. [8]

However, all these theories and techniques do not give
consideration to such extraeconomical factors as subsidies
and other incentives granted by governments to induce companies to locate in a particular region. A typical statement
designating certain regions as high-priority regions deserv-
ing of subsidies can be found in the following statement of the
third objective in the 1967 amendment of the Israel Law for
the Encouragement of Capital Investments:

> the absorption of immigration, the planned distri-
> bution of the population over the area of the State
> and the creation of new sources of employment[9]

To implement this objective, the Israeli government
divided the country into three priority areas. Investors in
priority areas A and B benefited from the high incentives described in Chapter 1, while investors in area C (the rest of
the country) did not benefit from the location subsidies. See
Figure 5 for the official division into priority regions.

Do subsidies really affect the location decision? Do the
various grants and incentives induce companies to locate in a
particular area? And if so, in what way does it affect the
management process decision? Obviously, those industries
that locate in high-priority development regions should not be
considered because the nature of their business (mining, for
instance) requires location in these areas. We are interested
in companies for which the natural location can be somewhere
else, or for whom the ideal location is not a priority development region.

Tables 12, 13, 14, and Figure 6 indicate a definite rise
in the percentage-approved investments locating in developing
regions. What is even more important is the drastic increase
in the magnitude of the investment in region A during 1967
compared with 1966 (see Table 15). The total investment in
developing regions rose from approximately $193 million in
1966 to $493 million in 1967, most of it going to development
region A where investments rose from $92 million in 1966 to
approximately $313 million in 1967. Indeed, the director of
the Israeli Investment Authority cites these figures in the introduction to the 1967 annual report[10] as valid proof of the

FIGURE 5

Priority Development Areas of Israel

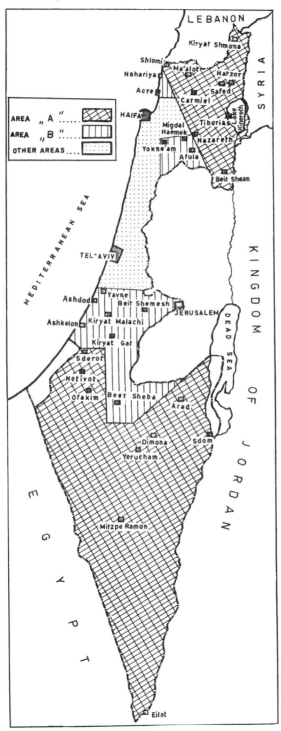

FIGURE 6

Approved Development Region Projects
as Percentage of Total Number of Approved Projects
Israel, 1962-1967

Source: Table 14.

48

TABLE 12

Approved New and Expansion Projects
by Industry Branch, Israel, 1962-67

BRANCH	1962	1963	1964	1965	1966	1967
Mining	1	--	--	--	1	1
Food	12	6	6	7	4	9
Textile	14	18	15	13	8	19
Clothing and Leather	1	9	11	3	8	9
Wood and Wood Products	3	5	3	4	7	15
Paper, Cardboard, Printing	3	1	3	3	6	6
Ceramics and Glass	1	6	1	6	1	1
Cement and Construction Products	8	3	4	4	1	--
Plastics	2	7	14	4	2	6
Rubber Products	1	1	2	1	1	1
Chemicals, Pharmaceuticals, Paints	5	10	11	12	7	13
Metal Products	6	16	16	12	14	18
Cars and Transportation	3	5	3	4	5	10
Mechanical Precision Products	1	3	--	--	2	2
Electrical Equipment	7	2	8	3	12	14
Other Manufacturing	12	6	17	14	11	19
Total Industry	80	98	114	90	90	143

Source: State of Israel Investment Authority, Israel Investment Authority Operations to December 31, 1965 (Jerusalem, January, 1966), p. 6; Israel Investment Authority Report for 1967 (Jerusalem, January, 1968), p. 13.

TABLE 13

Approved Projects in Priority Regions,
Israel, 1962-67

BRANCH	1962	1963	1964	1965	1966	1967
Mining	1	--	--	--	1	1
Food	8	3	4	4	4	7
Textile	8	9	7	7	5	14
Clothing and Leather	--	5	6	3	6	8
Wood and Wood Products	3	5	3	3	6	13
Paper, Cardboard, Printing	--	1	2	2	4	4
Ceramics and Glass	1	3	1	5	1	--
Cement and Construction Products	3	2	1	3	1	--
Plastics	2	6	10	3	2	4
Rubber Products	1	--	--	1	--	1
Chemicals, Pharmaceuticals, Paints	1	3	3	5	2	11
Metal Products	3	11	6	7	11	13
Cars and Transportation	1	1	3	4	4	7
Mechanical Precision Products	--	--	--	--	--	1
Electrical Equipment	1	--	2	2	8	11
Other Manufacturing	6	1	4	3	8	10
Total Industry	39	50	52	52	63	105

Source: State of Israel Investment Authority, Israel Investment Authority Operations to December 31, 1965 (Jerusalem, January, 1966), p. 6; Israel Investment Authority Report for 1967 (Jerusalem, January, 1968), p. 13.

TABLE 14

Percent Approved Projects in Priority Regions

YEAR	TOTAL APPROVED PROJECTS	APPROVED PROJECTS IN PRIORITY REGIONS	PERCENT APPROVALS TO PRIORITY REGIONS
1962	80	39	48.8
1963	90	50	55.6
1964	114	52	45.6
1965	90	52	57.8
1966	90	63	70.0
1967	143	105	72.5

Source: Table 12 and Table 13.

TABLE 15

Approved Projects by Priority Development Region, 1966-67

	NUMBER OF APPROVED PROJECTS			INVESTMENT IN APPROVED PROJECTS (ISRAELI POUNDS 1000)		
YEAR	A	B	TOTAL (A+B+ ALL OTHER)	A	B	TOTAL
1966	29	34	90	92,130	38,976	193,278
1967	42	63	143	312,705	152,257	493,291

Source: State of Israel Investment Authority, Israel Investment Authority Report for 1967 (Jerusalem, January, 1968), p. 13.

success of the April 12, 1967, amendment to the Law for the
Encouragement of Capital Investment which clearly divided
the country into the three priority regions and established the
available grants and incentives (see Chapter 1, Tables 2 and 3).
But a more careful analysis of the investments (Table 16) reveals that of the total $313 million invested in region A, $265
million were invested on new and expanded chemical plants in
the Dead Sea complex. These expenditures probably would
have been made regardless of the subsidies offered for locating
in region A as this region is the natural location for such an
investment. Likewise, in Table 17 it is obvious that the large
investment in region A was allocated for new equipment necessary for the development of the petro-chemical complex.

The arguments discussed earlier with respect to the effect of subsidies on the country selection decision are similar
to those arguments applied to the site selection decision. In
this case it may be argued that certain industries would locate
in development regions (the Dead Sea complex in the Israeli
example) because of the natural advantages of such regions,
and would do so regardless of the existence of subsidies. In
such cases subsidies are accepted because they exist.

Since the amendment providing cash grants and low-
interest loans for location in development regions is due to
expire in 1970, there are already debates as to whether or not
the law should be extended. The adherents of the subsidy system claim that the disproportionate rise in investment during
1967 and the apparently continuing trend in 1968 and 1969 is
due largely to the introduction of the above subsidies. On the
other hand, the opponents of this theory claim that the increase
is due to the existence of stable political and economic conditions that would have attracted investors anyway. It is evident from discussions with managers and investors in the
electronics industry and other manufacturing enterprises
associated with the Israeli defense establishment that the
companies accept the subsidies because they exist. Further-
more, they would still invest in the same industries should
these subsidies not exist.

An analogy can be made between subsidies to promote
export and subsidies for locating in specific regions. The
study on the export potential of the Israeli manufacturing
firms mentioned in an earlier chapter found that although
most exporting firms claimed that they would not be profit-
making without the subsidies, a high proportion indicated that
they would still continue to export should their subsidies be

TABLE 16

Total Investment in Industry by Branch and Region, Israel
1966-67

(in thousands of Israeli Pounds)

| | 1966 | | |
BRANCH	REGION A	REGION B	TOTAL
Mining	5,499	--	5,499
Food	7,059	10,450	17,509
Textile	7,000	1,973	12,532
Clothing and Leather	1,325	2,923	4,706
Wood and Wood Products	6,524	500	7,530
Paper, Cardboard, Printing	700	1,438	27,038
Ceramics and Glass	3,700	--	3,700
Cement and Construction Products	--	90	90
Plastics	1,050	--	1,050
Rubber Products	--	--	727
Chemicals, Pharmaceuticals, Paint	1,251	3,127	23,229
Metal Products	50,253	4,823	56,887
Cars and Transportation	--	4,152	8,152
Mechanical Precision Products	--	--	3,604
Electrical Equipment	310	8,575	10,946
Other Manufacturing	7,359	925	10,019
Total Industry	92,130	38,976	193,278

(continued)

53

TABLE 16 (continued)

BRANCH	1967		
	REGION A	REGION B	TOTAL
Mining	--	415	415
Food	302	8,129	9,638
Textile	17,582	25,087	50,498
Clothing and Leather	2,864	26,022	29,011
Wood and Wood Products	4,333	5,768	13,971
Paper, Cardboard, Printing	1,967	626	2,294
Ceramics and Glass	--	--	375
Cement and Construction Products	--	--	--
Plastics	2,595	423	4,282
Rubber Products	--	1,086	1,086
Chemicals, Pharmaceuticals, Paint	264,950	6,502	272,502
Metal Products	13,462	6,053	21,845
Cars and Transportation	1,597	53,205	57,251
Mechanical Precision Products	--	1,040	1,080
Electrical Equipment	1,597	14,036	19,740
Other Manufacturing	1,474	3,865	8,673
Total Industry	312,705	152,257	493,291

Source: State of Israel Investment Authority, Israel Investment Authority Report for 1967 (Jerusalem, January, 1968), p. 13.

54

TABLE 17

Allocation of Investment Capital,
Israel, 1967
(thousands of Israeli Pounds)

PURPOSE	REGION A	REGION B	OTHER REGIONS	TOTAL
Land and Development	1,580	2,456	510	4,546
Buildings	23,821	26,822	5,161	55,804
Equipment				
New	356,674	77,053	14,281	448,008
Used	1,311	1,412	225	2,948
Other General Expenses	70,972	13,513	5,733	90,218
Total Fixed Assets	454,358	121,256	25,918	601,524
Working Capital	36,927	24,682	6,290	67,899
Total	491,285	145,938	32,200	669,423

Source: State of Israel Investment Authority, Israel Investment Authority Report for 1967 (Jerusalem, January, 1968), p. 14.

discontinued.[11] The same is probably true with the plant location decision. Some will locate in a certain development
region because of the availability of subsidies while others
would locate there anyway and accept the subsidies since they
are entitled to them.

A careful look at the regional division map (Figure 5) and
a study of new and relocating companies indicates that there is
a trend toward concentrating on a certain segment of region B
within a range of no more than 50 miles from the two largest
markets and population centers, and in most cases no more
than 25 miles from these centers (the Dan Bloc and Jerusalem).
The reason for this concentration is very simple: The major
urban areas, Tel Aviv, Haifa, and Jerusalem, exhibit all the
disadvantages of plant location in an urban area such as high
land cost, zoning laws, and lack of room for expansion. A
new or expanding company facing the problem of acquiring
new land is confronted with the prohibitive costs of locating
or expanding in these areas. Consequently, they must move
to the outer limits and even beyond the city limits. If, following this reasoning, a company decides to move 10 to 15 miles
away from the urban area, then they may as well add another
10 miles, locate in the nearest development region, and take
advantage of the subsidies granted for locating there.

The other type of investors make an a priori decision
that they want to benefit from the subsidies, and then decide
to locate within the development region. But they will still
try to pick a site close to the ideal site assuming it is not
in a developing region. For example, a certain manufacturer
explained that he had chosen to establish his company in
Yavneh because it happens to be the nearest alternative to
the ideal location; namely, Lydda. Some of these companies
tend to forego their long-range considerations for quick earnings and a fast return on their investments.

It is understandable that companies with high cost of capital, that is, those employing a high-discount factor in capital-
izing their future earnings, will obviously emphasize the near
cash flow in a development region rather than distant flows in
the future. Since in addition to cash grants and loans these
companies benefit for a limited period (five years) from exemptions or lowered income tax rates, both the short-run and
break-even analyses will show a lower break-even point, and
the net profit will be equal to or close to the difference between
revenue and sales (see Figure 7). In this particular example
a hypothetical break-even chart is employed. Break-even
analysis, despite its limited applicability as a static model for

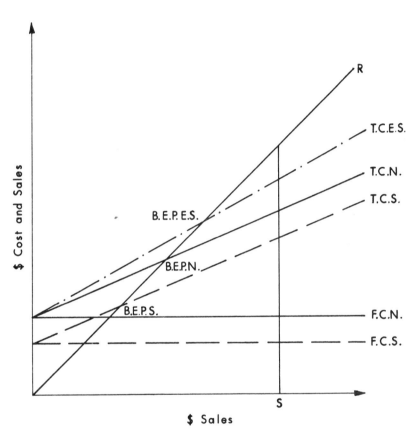

FIGURE 7

The Impact of Subsidies on Break-Even Analysis

B.E.P.N.   : Break-Even-Point, Normal
B.E.P.S.   : Break-Even-Point, Subsidy
F.C.N.   : Fixed Cost, Normal
F.C.S.   : Fixed Cost, Subsidy
T.C.S.   : Total Cost, Subsidy
T.C.N.   : Total Cost, Normal
B.E.P.E.S. : Break-Even-Point, End Subsidy
T.C.E.S.   : Total Cost, End Subsidy

R : Revenue
S : Sales

short-run relationships, linearity assumptions, the dependence of profit on output only, and the continuation of the same relative sales and expense patterns, is nevertheless one of the more popular tools employed in the location decision. In this particular use it renders an inexpensive picture as to the relative break-even point of the various alternatives under consideration. In the location decision, firms usually choose the alternative with the lowest break-even point (other factors not being considered).[12] This same criterion is illustrated in Figure 7 and in the following discussion. For any given sales volume (S) regardless whether a firm is exempt or has to pay 50 percent income, its profit will be higher for at least as long as the subsidies continue. It is assumed in Figure 7 that variable costs remain unchanged for the two locations. This assumption is not practical since in reality variable costs such as transportation, wages, and salaries are usually greater for the developing region. Hence, if we assume a return to normal fixed costs for the development region location (although fixed costs often increase by the need to establish central offices in the major cities), the higher variable costs will tend to shift the break-even point to a higher level and both gross and net income will decrease. The investor evaluates the alternatives by methods such as are discussed in Chapter 2, that is, the present value, or the equivalent annual cost method. If he is interested in receiving a quick return on his investment, he may forego long-run consideration and be satisfied with a short-run analysis as long as he achieves his prime goal; namely, immediate cash flow. At the end of the tax and subsidy holiday he may decide it is no longer lucrative to continue operations. He may then discontinue operations and become a casualty on the Investment Authority list. Meanwhile, the government and the economy will bear the brunt of his unsuccessful speculative venture.

Are the location subsidies at least affective in achieving their prime goals; namely, the spreading of population and the creation of employment? It can be said that by keeping within a radius of about fifty miles from the major urban areas, these subsidies may at best help in thinning the heavy population layer in the center. But as long as factories are built within commuter's reach, employees will tend to remain at their present location, thus avoiding the problems of relocation and continuing to take advantage of the sociocultural aspects of the large city. As to the creation of employment, this subject will be discussed in the following chapter.

NOTES

1. R. B. Stobaugh, "Where in the World Should We Put That Plant?", Harvard Business Review, January-February, 1969, p. 129.

2. Ibid.

3. For an illustrative example of the application of the point system see Ibid.

4. For China, see Council for International Economic Cooperation and Development, Foreign Investment and Trade--Republic of China (Taipei, April, 1967); for Korea, see Office of Investment Promotion, Investment Guide to Korea (Seoul, 1967), p. 31; for Israel, see Table 11.

5. CBS News, Friday, April 11, 1969.

6. A. Lösch, The Economics of Location (New York: John Wiley and Sons, 1967), p. 16.

7. J. H. von Thünen, Der Isolierte Staat in Beziehung auf Landwirtschaft und Nationalokonomie (Hamburg, Ger., 1826); Alfred Weber, Ueber den Standort der Industrien (Tubingen, Ger., 1909); Tord Palander, Beitrage zur Standortstheorie (Uppsala, Ger., 1935).

8. Lösch, op. cit. pp. 16-35.

9. State of Israel Investment Authority, Law for the Encouragement of Capital Investments (Jerusalem, January, 1967), p. 12.

10. State of Israel Investment Authority, Israel Investment Authority Report for 1967 (Jerusalem, January, 1968).

11. S. Hirsch, The Export Potential of Israeli Manufacturing Enterprises (Tel Aviv:-Israel Management Institute, 1968), p. 16.

12. For a discussion of break-even analysis see Walter Rautenstrauch and Raymond Villers, The Economics of Industrial Management, 2nd ed. (New York: Funk and Wagnalls, 1957).

CHAPTER **4** THE TECHNOLOGY
DECISION

One of the important decisions that industrial firms face
everywhere is the choice of the particular level of technology
at which to operate. The term "level of technology" usually
refers to the state of the art of an industry at a given time.
Most often this expression refers to the choice of production
methods and in this particular interpretation it will be employed in this chapter. Several of the subsidy systems listed
in Chapter 1 are designed to influence this choice. It will be
the major objective of this chapter to investigate how the level
of technology decision is affected by the subsidy factor.

It is common to identify the function of industrial management with the task of coordinating men, materials, machines,
and money in an efficient manner. With respect to the cost of
materials and the availability of finance, management may have
only limited flexibility. On the other hand, the design and
choice of the desired man-machine ratio is often an operational
decision entirely under management control. Management often
has an option to choose any feasible technology level among
the many alternatives, from the labor-intensive to the capital-
intensive method of operation.

The choice, of course, is limited to the number of alternatives available. Some products may require a specific
process with high initial costs and with little or no flexibility
whatsoever in the combination of labor and equipment. Some
chemical processes are examples of this kind. When the cost
of the operation is only secondary in significance, the decision
of whether or not to invest may rely upon factors other than
economic feasibility. Defense industries are examples of this
kind.

However, wherever alternative techniques and processes
exist there are indications that capital-intensive methods are
utilized. Even in areas where relative manpower costs would
indicate a rational choice of more labor-intensive operations,
such methods are used despite the goal to create employment
in such areas. It is not the intent of this discussion to

investigate reasons for unemployment and relative low labor
costs in such areas, nor is it the intent to explore the complex
set of factors forming the basis for preference of capital-
intensive techniques. Rather, the impact of one particular factor, namely, subsidies, will be examined, as its allocation
affects the cost of equipment, thereby influencing the level of
technology decision.

There are many types of subsidies, and it is practically
impossible to separate them and their individual impact on the
firm, for none of the various types of subsidies discussed so
far acts exclusively towards the attainment of a desired goal.
It is rather the combined effect of all these subsidies that leaves
its imprint on the economy. Consequently, we may conceive
of subsidies acting in opposing directions with respect to a
certain aim, or of subsidies intended to promote a given objective having at the same time a negative effect on another
desired goal or criterion.

A case in point is the seeming contradiction between the
objective to create employment in development regions, and
hence promote labor-intensive industries, and the criteria of
economic feasibility and production for export. In Israel this
conflict is due mainly to the existence of two factors that shall
be demonstrated in Tables 18-22. On the one hand, wages for
labor in Israel are relatively high and keep increasing at a
consistent rate as shown in Tables 18 and 19. On the other
hand, labor productivity is increasing at a much slower rate,
as seen in Tables 20 and 21.

These conditions, coupled with the fact that wages in Israel
are comparatively higher than in other countries, [1] caused production costs of labor-intensive enterprises to be higher than
the production costs of comparable foreign industries. This
rise in labor costs, combined with the resulting inability to
compete with foreign manufacturers due to excessive operational costs, led management to seek alternative methods of
operation.

Management response to the phenomenon of rising alternative costs followed Professor S. Melman's theory on
industrial labor productivity. [2] After examining the ratio of
labor to machine costs it was found that labor costs increased
continuously and at a high rate, while the index of the relative
price of equipment dropped from 100 points in 1962 to 71 points
in 1966, as evident from Table 22. Management chose to
mechanize.

The decision to mechanize was further strengthened by the
fact that throughout the years the cost of electrical power for

TABLE 18

Average Monthly Salary and Percentage Change
in the Average Monthly Salary per Worker
in Industry, Crafts, Mines, and Quarries,
Israel, 1962-66

YEAR	AVERAGE MONTHLY SALARIES (Israeli pounds)		PERCENTAGE CHANGE IN AVERAGE MONTHLY SALARIES	
	ALL EM-PLOYEES	PERMANENT EMPLOYEES	ALL EM-PLOYEES	PERMANENT EMPLOYEES
1961	278	292	--	--
1962	310	325	11.4	11.7
1963	349	363	12.6	11.7
1964	392	410	12.3	12.7
1965	460	477	16.2	15.2
1966	538	557	17.0	16.8

Source: Central Bureau of Statistics, Statistical Abstract
of Israel 1967, 18 (Jerusalem, 1968), pp. 298-300.

TABLE 19

Wages and Salaries in Manufacturing (Indexes)
(base: average 1958 = 100.0)

YEAR	WAGES AND SALARIES OF EMPLOYEES	WAGES AND SALARIES OF WORKERS	WORKER'S NOMINAL DAILY WAGE	WORKER'S REAL DAILY WAGE
1959	114	114	104	103
1960	128	126	108	104
1961	158	155	117	106
1962	192	188	130	107
1963	234	228	144	112
1964	274	268	159	117
1965	318	308	182	125
1966	360	347	212	134

Source: Central Bureau of Statistics, Statistical Abstract
of Israel 1967, 18 (Jerusalem, 1968), pp. 386-389.

TABLE 20

Percentage Increase in Wages, Output, and
Ratio of Capital to Output and Ratio of
Average Monthly Wages to Output,
Israel, 1961-66

YEAR	PERCENT IN-CREASE IN WAGES[1]	PERCENT IN-CREASE IN OUTPUT[2]	RATIO OF CAPITAL TO OUT-PUT[3]	RATIO OF AVERAGE MONTHLY WAGES TO OUTPUT[4]
1961	--	--	0.66	0.14
1962	11.4	3.4	0.65	0.15
1963	12.6	4.9	0.65	0.16
1964	12.3	8.2	0.63	0.17
1965	16.2	8.0	0.63	0.18
1966	17.0	3.7	0.65	0.21

[1]From Table 18.
[2]Control Bureau of Statistics, Statistical Abstract of Israel 1967, 18 (Jerusalem, 1968), p. 407.
[3]Ibid., p. 405.
[4]Calculated by dividing average monthly salaries in Table 19 by output per worker divided by 12 in Table 21.

industrial use had increased only slightly, and for the period 1966-69, it remained at an average of 3.31 Agorot per KWH (approximately 0.95 cents per KWH). [3]

That management chose to mechanize is evident from the increase in industrial power consumption, as shown in Table 23, from the continuous growth of capital outlays per employed person in industry, and especially from the rates of growth of these outlays during 1961-66, as demonstrated in Table 24. One of the effects derived from the decision to mechanize and adopt capital-intensive means of production was the increase in productivity per employed person as seen in Table 21.

What role have subsidies played in the decision to mechanize? No doubt the availability of capital grants for equipment and buildings in priority development regions, as shown in

TABLE 21

Employment and Output per Worker in Industry,
Israel, 1950-66

YEAR	EMPLOYEES (thousand)	AVERAGE ANNUAL INCREASE (percent)	INDUSTRIAL EMPLOY-MENT AS PERCENT OF ALL PERSONS EMPLOYED	OUTPUT PER WORKER (at 1966 prices in thousands of Israeli pounds)
1950	89.4	--	21.2	16.2
1951	107.4	20.1	20.9	14.2
1952	109.2	1.7	20.1	13.5
1953	111.7	2.3	20.2	14.5
1954	121.5	8.8	21.9	15.3
1955	124.0	2.1	21.5	16.9
1956	130.0	4.8	21.9	17.7
1957	138.8	6.8	21.6	19.0
1958	146.7	5.7	22.4	19.7
1959	153.7	4.8	22.6	21.2
1960	162.9	6.0	23.2	22.5
1961	177.8	9.1	24.2	23.7
1962	194.7	9.5	25.1	24.5
1963	210.4	8.1	25.8	25.7
1964	221.6	5.3	25.9	27.8
1965	224.5	1.3	25.5	30.0
1966	222.0	-1.1	25.3	31.1

Source: Economic Planning Authority, Israel's Economic Development: Past Progress and Plan for the Future (Jerusalem, March, 1968), p. 407.

Tables 1 and 2 in Chapter 1 significantly enticed management
to select more capital-intensive means of production. However,
the data for wages, relative equipment price, and the cost of
electrical power (Tables 22 and 23) indicates that management
would have probably chosen the same course of action, namely, more mechanization, as a logical consequence of rising labor costs. Subsidies decreased the relative price of equipment,
thereby making the choice of capital-intensive methods more
obvious. This particular point is substantiated by the fact that
capital investment per employed person in approved enterprises
entitled to subsidies was three to four times larger than the
capital per gainfully employed person in industry as a whole.
In addition data available for the two years since the formal
establishment of priority development regions indicates that
capital investments per employed person in these regions tend
to be even higher. These last two facts are demonstrated in
Tables 24 and 25.

The data available for the development regions (see Table
25) may be misleading as the approved investment of approximately IL456 million (1967) includes a major outlay of close
to IL265 million for the expansion of the Dead Sea industrial
complex. Should this particular investment be removed from
the total, the capital outlay would be IL200 million for 6,448
employees or IL31,000 per employee. This figure is still
about 50 percent higher than the equivalent figure for industry
as a whole, as demonstrated in Table 24 for the year 1966.

It is interesting to note that the creation of employment
for an additional 430 persons necessitated an investment of
IL265 million, or IL615,000 per additional employee. This
high figure is due to the unusually high initial investment required by the petro-chemical industry whose processes require
a capital-intensive operation.

This phenomenon of relatively high capital investment per
employee in development regions is to a large extent a direct
result of the reduction in equipment cost and one effect of
subsidies. If the purpose of these subsidies was to create employment by inducing labor-intensive firms to locate in these
regions then it may be said that the results, at least in the
case of Israel, show only partial success. The number of jobs
created is a significant criterion in awarding the various government grants and loans. However, the importance of this factor
seems to diminish when management has to allow for normal
considerations, such as alternative costs, to prevail. And indeed, a look at the employment distribution in Figure 8 clearly depicts the sparcity of employment in the priority development regions despite the subsidy systems.

TABLE 22

Index of the Price of Industrial Equipment
Relative to the Price of Labor, 1962-66

YEAR	INDEX OF NOMINAL HOURLY WAGES IN INDUSTRY	INDEX OF INDUSTRIAL EQUIPMENT PRICES	INDEX OF THE RELATIVE PRICE OF EQUIPMENT
1962	100	100	100
1963	112	106	95
1964	124	108	87
1965	137	111	81
1966	159	113	71

Source: Bank of Israel, Annual Report 1966 (Jerusalem, May, 1967), p. 115.

TABLE 23

Electrical Power Consumption by
Israeli Industry
(in million kwh)

YEAR		MILLION KWH PER 1000 EMPLOYEES	AVERAGE YEARLY INCREASE (percent)
1956	350	2.7	
1961	796	4.5	17.9 (1956-61)
1966	1,253	5.7	9.5 (1961-66)
1967	1,390		
1971 (pro- jected)	2,000		9.8 (1966-71)

Source: Economic Planning Authority, Israel's Economic Development: Past Progress and Plan for the Future (Jerusalem, March, 1968), pp. 430-433.

TABLE 24

Capital Stock per Gainfully Employed
Person in Industry, Mining, and Quarrying,
Israel, 1950-67
(at 1966 prices)

YEAR	CAPITAL PER EMPLOYED PERSON (Israeli pounds)	GROWTH OF CAPITAL PER EMPLOYED PERSON (percent)
1950	6,540	--
1951	6,890	5.4
1952	8,910	29.3
1953	10,430	17.1
1954	10,650	2.1
1955	11,600	8.8
1956	12,120	4.6
1957	12,750	5.2
1958	13,300	4.3
1959	14,330	7.7
1960	15,550	8.5
1961	15,700	1.0
1962	15,980	1.7
1963	16,750	4.8
1964	17,600	5.1
1965	18,850	7.1
1966	20,160	6.9

Source: Economic Planning Authority, Israel's Economic
Development: Past Progress and Plan for the Future
(Jerusalem, March, 1968), p. 405.

TABLE 25

Approved Capital Stock per Employed
Person in Industry, Israel, 1963-67

YEAR	APPROVED INVESTMENTS (in thousands of Israeli pounds)	ESTIMATED NUMBER OF EMPLOYEES	CAPITAL OUTLAY PER EMPLOYEE
1963	180,449	4,682	38,800
1964	261,581	5,276	49,700
1965	222,252	5,049	44,200
1966	255,710	3,371	75,500
1967	676,093	7,671	88,100
DEVELOPMENT REGION			
1966	131,106	2,339	56,200
1967	464,962	6,778	68,700
OTHER REGIONS			
1966	62,172	1,032	60,000
1967	28,329	893	31,700

Source: State of Israel Investment Authority, Israel Investment Authority Report for 1967 (Jerusalem, January, 1968), pp. 7, 12, 13; Israel Investment Authority Operations to December 31, 1965 (Jerusalem, January, 1966), Tables 7 and 8.

FIGURE 8

Employed Persons in Industry and Crafts
by Natural and Development Region
(Absolute Numbers)

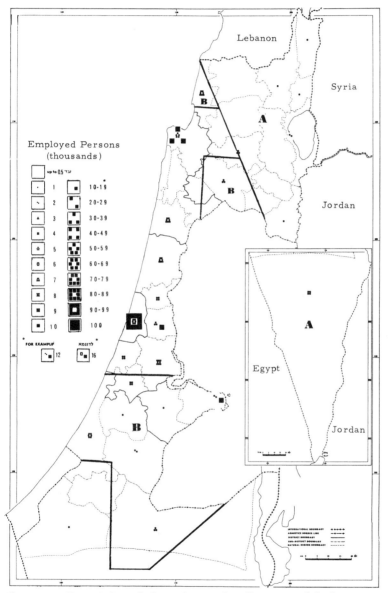

Source: Provisional data from the Census of Industry and Crafts, 1965 (Central Bureau of Statistics, Jerusalem, 1966).

69

In Figure 8 the straight black lines divide the country according to priority development regions as defined in Figure 5. The small black squares dispersed throughout the map represent the number of persons employed in the respective regions following the scale on the left side of the map. It is quite obvious that the number of employed persons in industry and crafts in development regions A and B is relatively small, despite government efforts to generate employment in those regions.

Another consideration in the decision to mechanize is the limited market of semiskilled and skilled labor in the development areas. Even though labor wages in Israel are relatively high, the salaries of skilled technicians and professionals is significantly lower than in other developed countries.[4] (An engineer grade A with ten years seniority earns $400 per month.) Naturally, it would seem that science-based industries would be able to take advantage of this fact. Indeed, in recent years a few science-based industry parks have taken shape, but they are not in development regions where employment is needed, but near institutions of higher education and research where such manpower resources are logically located. Attempts are made to try to attract skilled personnel to development regions via other types of subsidies (lower income tax, higher salaries), but these incentives usually are not sufficient to balance the advantages otherwise found in nondevelopment regions.

But whenever higher salaries succeed in drawing skilled employees to development regions, there is a rise in production costs and the comparative advantage of lower wages is lost, again reducing the practicality of competition on foreign markets.

Thus far, we have emphasized one phenomenon associated with the impact of subsidies on technology decisions; namely, the significantly higher capital per employee ratio. We have explained that subsidies granted for the acquisition of equipment have the effect of lowering equipment costs. This reduction in equipment costs, in turn, leads management towards more mechanization. In addition to mechanization, subsidies offer management two more options. Rather than shifting towards a higher degree of mechanization, from manual to automated equipment, for example, management may choose to increase the capacity of operations by just adding equipment at the same level of technology. Or, management may utilize a subsidy for the achievement of both a higher level of technology and a larger capacity. A shift from manual to semiautomatic equipment rather than to fully automated equipment is an example of such utilization. Such movements to a new level of technology are represented in Figure 9.

FIGURE 9

Capital-Labor Proportion
in Various Processes*

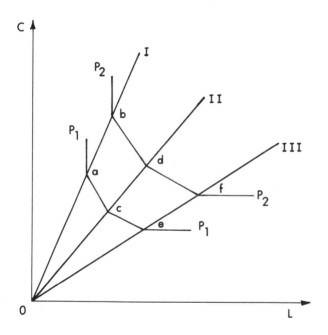

C – Capital

L – Labor

Lines I, II, and III represent alternatives for constant product-processes.

Lines P_1, P_2 represent productivity levels, $P_2 > P_1$.

Points a, c, e and b, d, f represent the alternative combination of factors that can be used to represent an equal volume of output P_1 and P_2 respectively.

Given just one possible process, process I, any change
in price ratio (L/M) will permit movement along one expansion
path only; namely, Oab. In other words, should the relative
price index of equipment decline more, capital-intensive
methods of manufacturing will be employed. Consequently,
an increase in productivity, or at least in the available capacity for output is derived. It is intuitively understandable that
such subsidies as grants towards the purchase of new equipment have the effect of further lowering the relative equipment
cost to the investor, again justifying a capital-intensive investment. On the other hand, should more than one process-
technology be available, such as process I, II, and III, then
movement is also possible from one process to another. Assume that the factor combination C is used for output level
P_1. If it becomes desirable to increase output to level P_2
management is no more restrained in keeping the same factor
proportion and moving along path Ocd to point d. It may consider shifting to either combination f or b, both on the equal
output line P_2. This possible shift will again be a function of
the relative factor price ratio. Should the relative index of
equipment cost decrease as demonstrated in the case of Israel
(see Table 22), management will tend to move towards the
capital-intensive process, process I and factor combination
b in our illustration. Again, as in the single process case,
subsidies will have the effect of lowering the relative equipment cost and indirectly serving as an incentive for a more
capital-intensive operation, even though, as suggested earlier,
the purpose of these subsidies may be the creation of employment. Again, as in the case of the single process industry,
the new technology may create a higher productive capacity,
not necessarily required by existing market opportunity.

This fact together with economy-of-scale considerations
also may be the reason for the excessive capacity (e. g., the
plastics industry at 60 percent of capacity)[5] which causes a
high degree of equipment under-utilization, with all the associated overhead and fixed costs a burden on the profitability of
the enterprise. These two phenomena were not thoroughly
researched in this volume; such research needs a more detailed and careful examination of each enterprise and industry,
its associated methods of production, and its feasible scales of
operation.

NOTES

1. M. Bruno, "Productivity and Rates of Return in Israel--1952-61," Economic Quarterly, 37/38 (Tel Aviv, March, 1963).

2. Seymour Melman, Dynamic Factors in Industrial Productivity (New York: John Wiley and Sons, 1956), p. 3.

3. State of Israel Investment Authority, Israel Investors' Manual (Jerusalem, 1968), pp. 81-82.

4. Ibid., pp. 55-62.

5. Ministry of Commerce and Industry, Surveys of Israeli Industries, prepared for the Economic Conference of April, 1968 (Jerusalem, February, 1968).

CHAPTER 5

THE SUBSIDY-MAXIMIZING FIRM

In the preceding chapters the effects of subsidy programs on managerial decisions were analyzed. These decisions were judged according to the regularly accepted criteria of engineering economy. Subsidies were viewed as an additional, sometimes new, factor to be considered in the decision-making process. Under these criteria the manufacturing firm was regarded as a profit-maximizing institution, [1] and the subsidies when their effect on the profits of the firm was small were of little importance.

But the existence of a variety of subsidy programs, as described in Chapter 1, gave rise to another type of firm--the firm whose survival heavily depends upon the continuous receipt of subsidies; the firm which shows no viability without such subsidies. Such a firm will still strive for profits, but profits in this case are realized on quite a different basis. While the normal industrial firm will survive and profit through the right combination of market demand, product quality, price, cost of production, efficiency of operations, and other factors that bring success to a manufacturing organization, the heavily subsidized firm derives most of its income and profit from various subsidy programs. Hence, the major goal of such a firm is to optimize its overall returns by finding that level of performance which will entitle it to a steady and continous flow of subsidy benefits.

Since this income is not a result of the normal functions of a productive organization, the resulting level of performance for such a subsidy-maximizing firm is not the efficient operational performance of the normal profit-maximizing firm. It is even conceivable for the subsidy-maximizing firms to prefer operating at a low level of efficiency, if this inefficiency ensures them subsidy benefits larger than the profits which they might derive from a more efficient operation. In such a case management will consider the loss of a given subsidy more detrimental to the survival of the firm than some inefficiencies, the removal of which may cause the discontinuation of the subsidy. When such conditions exist it seems that subsidies are to some extent premiums for inefficiency, as cost minimization is not a prerequisite to subsidy maximization.

But how does such a firm come into existence? How is the subsidy-maximizing firm established and what are the mechanics that allow it to survive? The answer to these questions must be sought on two separate levels. One is the investor or firm level, that is, the beneficiary of the subsidy programs; the other is the governmental level, or the donor side.

THE INVESTOR

In Chapter 2 the impact of subsidy programs on several investment-decision criteria was analyzed. That analysis did not look for the possible motives of such investors but rather at the logic used to justify investments under a subsidy program incentive. Nevertheless, it is possible to distinguish at least two types of investors here. There is the firm with a good product and with an efficient production organization that accepts a subsidy in order to expand or relocate and to avoid taking a loan. Such companies will limit the size of the subsidy they may accept if they do not wish the government to acquire a vested interest in the company which could eventually lead to sustained interference with the management of the organization. These companies will continue to maintain their autonomy and make their own decisions, while seeking to maximize profits by the normal methods available to a manufacturing firm. The viability of such firms does not depend on subsidies, and operational efficiency will not be sacrificed to ensure the continuous flow of subsidy benefits. But companies of this kind are exceptions among companies seeking subsidies. It is more common to find the second type of company, one whose original investment purpose was aimed at the manipulation of subsidy systems and whose goal is the optimization of subsidy returns. These companies become a burden on the nation's economy, but governments find it difficult to disengage themselves. Their involvement is due to the vested interest which has developed over years of subsidization.

How is the subsidy-maximizing company established, and even more important, how does it continue to survive once it has been established? This question is quite relevant to this discussion since, as was suggested in Chapter 2, subsidized companies show a very low mortality rate. To answer these questions an attempt will be made to follow through the various alternative strategies available to a potential investor desirous of taking advantage of existing subsidy programs.

Basically, the entire development process may be divided into three time intervals, in which each interval is characterized by a certain strategy. First, there is the preoperational period which begins with the investment idea and ends when the firm is ready to start production. The average time interval for this period is one to three years. During the first period the investor employs a strategy that enables him to invest the minimal capital required to obtain the various cash grants and loans at the reduced interest rate. Once he obtains this share of government capital he starts using it in short-term, speculative investments--investments other than the one for which purpose the subsidy originally was granted.[2] By lending money at normal interest rates he already gains the difference between the normal rate and the reduced rate at which the capital was given to him. In reality the subsidy capital will be utilized in more risky ventures which may yield larger gains. It is obvious that such subsidy manipulators desire to extend the preproduction period as long as possible since an early investment in the building and acquisition of plant and equipment limits their speculative capability with the subsidy capital. Consequently, the heavily subsidized firms will exhibit a larger time-lag between the decision to invest and the actual start of production. After all possible delays have been exhausted and the government applies pressure on the investor to carry out the proposed investment plan and establish a productive enterprise the firm begins operations. Thus starts the second phase of the subsidy-maximizing strategy.

Once the firm is operating, a new selection of subsidies is available to an infant firm over a limited period of time, usually five years, to enable it to become conventionally profitable. Tax holidays, loans for working capital, and accelerated depreciations belong to this class of subsidies. The strategy employed by management during this infancy period will be to try to recoup their investment in the shortest pay-back period possible by optimizing the income from both the productive aspect of the firm and from the combined array of subsidy programs at its disposal. The tactics employed to this effect will involve the plant location and the level of technology decision. As suggested in Chapters 3 and 4 these decisions usually lead to location in development regions which in many cases would not be the natural choice of the conventional nonsubsidy-dependent firm. In addition these decisions

lead to either a higher level of technology, an excessive productive capacity, or to both. While the conventional profit-
maximizing firm seeks the best possible location according to
normally accepted criteria such as market proximity, raw
materials, labor cost, and transportation costs, and seeks to
utilize the early years of its operational life to free its production system of its various inefficiencies, sometimes even
accepting losses or reduced profits, the subsidy-maximizing
firm lays the foundations through the tactics described above
for its future inefficiency.

At the end of the second phase--the tax holiday period--it
is expected that the firm should be conventionally successful
and the danger of a reduction in subsidies confronts management. If indeed the firm is successful despite the tactics employed in the first two phases, then the reduction or even the
cessation of subsidies would not be detrimental to the firm's
operations; but such cases are the exception. As discussed
in Chapter 3 it is more common for such firms to have reached
an irreversible degree of internal inefficiency that any reduction in the subsidy benefits would endanger their viability. (This
situation is demonstrated by Figure 7, Chapter 3, when the
termination of subsidies creates a higher break-even point.)

The conventional industrial firm under similar conditions
would cease to exist, but this is not the case with the subsidized
firm; it still has some untapped subsidy programs available.
Now the firm is in the third phase--the maturity or post-tax
holiday period; the firm is operating inefficiently and subsidies
are needed to complement its normal income. Management
will now adapt its production so as to become entitled to any
subsidy programs not thus far used. The most common subsidies sought during this stage are the export subsidies. Again
the strategy adopted will be to optimize the combined production
and subsidy income. The tactics employed in pursuit of this
strategy will involve allocating part of the resources to the
production of a product which can be exported to foreign markets.
In many cases a new product will have to be introduced and
wherever the product is already on the company's manufacturing line a major quality-control program will have to be insti-
tuted. Only that segment of the firm's operations which is essential to the inflow of subsidies will be converted to export
manufacturing; the remainder will continue to operate along
the established lines. Although success is oftentimes within
reach through the adaptation of efficient methods of production,
it is conceivable that management will opt for the steady stream
of subsidies, rather than risk their reduction or termination.

Thus, situations are created whereby subsidies promote managerial incompetency and the continuation of industrial inefficiency. The strategies and tactics which lead to such situations are summarized in Figure 10.

Now that the managerial decision process which leads to the subsidy-maximizing idea has been described, it is relevant to focus attention on the characteristics of the responsible decision-makers, as these characteristics serve as background to the development of the subsidy-maximizing idea.

THE DONOR

Associated with the management of the subsidy-maximizing firm we observe two interesting phenomena. One is derived from the fact that a large proportion of the subsidies listed and classified in Chapter 1 is designed to draw foreign investments. As suggested earlier in this chapter one can imagine a potential investor with limited capital (and often without ideas) searching for an opportunity to invest who is attracted by the possibilities afforded by subsidy systems described thus far and who is willing to commit his capital towards the establishment of a subsidy-maximizing firm. But owner-investors rarely join the firm themselves and a new class of investors is encouraged by the subsidy system--a class of absentee investors.

In addition to the development of absentee investors, a new class of managers and investment consultants emerges. The major characteristic and qualification of this group is their specific ability to help establish and manage subsidy-maximizing firms. There are no exact figures of actual number of investment consultants, but a survey of the Israeli market showed an increase in the last 10 years. In the late 1950's and early 1960's there were only a handful of people engaged in the advise-giving profession. In recent years, however, with the formalization of investment procedures and the development of a fairly complex bureaucratic establishment, the "Investment Authority" with its formalized procedures and regulations, the number of investment consultants advising potential investors in Israel has increased extensively. It is estimated that there are some 2,000 such consultants. For Israel, with a total population of approximately 2.7 million, this figure is rather high.

In addition to the natural source of consulting personnel, the academic halls of the various institutions of higher learning and especially the graduate schools for business administration and industrial management, a large portion of the investment consultants and managers of subsidized firms in Israel are graduates of the subsidy-system complex, that is, former employees and executives of investment offices and departments of the finance and industrial development ministries previously associated with the government decision-making process in approving and granting incentives.

An inquiry as to the fate of former executives of the Investment Authority Office in New York revealed that, upon their return to Israel at the end of their official tour of duty in the United States, most of them found it more lucrative to turn to the investment consulting business and to manage the interests of absentee investors rather than continue in government employment. Some chose to stay in New York for the same purpose. The main asset of these individuals is not their ability to evaluate various alternatives and render an opinion as to what alternatives should be preferred, nor is it an expertise in industrial management, but rather it is their success in cutting through red tape and making the necessary contacts at the decision-making level of the bureaucratic hierarchy. Hence, they can probably get for their clients better conditions and almost always quicker results during the organization process, and continuous subsidies at the later stages.

In some ways an analogy may be drawn with the United States Military firm where the retired army officer serves as the link between the decision-making body of the Department of Defense and the marketing department of the firm he represents. In our case we substitute the ex-Investment Authority executive for the retired officer, but usually the former has more decision power. While the retired army officer usually promotes a product or tries to obtain a contract without actually being involved in the operational decisions of the firm he represents, the investment consultant at the formative stage and the firm executive at the later stages are directly involved in the decisions most crucial to the success of the firm.

Unless a potential investor has a well-defined project in his mind, or has the know-how for developing a certain product, he will have to resort to the advice of such consultant-managers. Consequently, decisions such as where to locate, what to produce, and what production techniques to employ are all left to be worked out between the former government executive, presently consultant or manager of the firm, and the present government executive.

In other words, decision-making is transferred from the capital investor to a group representing the combined interests

FIGURE 10

The Subsidy-Maximizing Versus the Profit-Maximizing Firm

I
THE PREPRODUCTION PHASE--
1-3 YEARS

THE SUBSIDY-
MAXIMIZING
FIRM

Strategy
1. Maximize immediate gains from available subsidy capital

Tactics
1. Minimize equity capital
2. Obtain maximum subsidy rate
3. Manipulate subsidy capital for largest and quickest returns
4. Maximize lead-time from obtainment of subsidy capital to actual investment in plant and equipment

THE PROFIT-
MAXIMIZING
FIRM

Strategy
1. Minimize necessary investment

Tactics
1. Minimize high-interest loans
2. Minimize subsidies
3. Minimize lead-time to production phase

II
INFANCY PHASE--
5 YEARS

THE SUBSIDY-
MAXIMIZING
FIRM

Strategy
1. Obtain largest and quickest returns from the combined subsidy-production phase

Tactics
1. Locate in development region
2. Aim at high capital/employee ratio--mechanize
3. Utilize all available subsidy benefits
4. Limit operational efficiency so as not to risk reduction or loss of subsidies

THE PROFIT-
MAXIMIZING
FIRM

Strategy
1. Become profitable as soon as possible

Tactics
1. Locate at best location
2. Select best means of production
3. Maximize overall operational efficiency

III
MATURITY PHASE

THE SUBSIDY-
MAXIMIZING
FIRM

Strategy
1. Seek continuity of subsidies

Tactics
1. Try to qualify for new types of subsidies such as export subsidies
2. Increase government interests in company by
   (a) large government financial support
   (b) cater for essential industry (defense)
   (c) bankruptcy - unemployment

THE PROFIT-
MAXIMIZING
FIRM

Strategy
1. Growth and expansion

Tactics
1. New products
2. New markets
3. New techniques
4. Cost-effectiveness programs

of the government--or subsidy donors--and subsidy manipulators, the beneficiaries of the subsidy programs.

The result is the establishment of a plant under conditions satisfactory to both parties. The government official thus justifies his employment by being able to show the investment he has attracted, and the consultant shows the subsidies and incentives he was able to obtain for the investor. Whether the end product of these sometimes conflicting aspirations is the best conceivable alternative is doubtful.

In Israel, as suggested in Chapter 2, the results of such machinations were not too gratifying and eventually led to the government crackdown on parasite industries during the slowdown period of 1965-67. That such action was necessary can be demonstrated from the facts revealed in a Bank of Israel study investigating changes in the financial structure of Israel's industrial companies. This study established that from the 1,493 industrial companies operating in 1956, only 10 companies declared bankruptcy by 1960.[3] No doubt many more companies were in financial difficulty but managed to drag on and avoid outright bankruptcy because of government assistance through various grants and loans. It is difficult to assess the magnitude of the government's involvement with marginal industrial companies in their quest for survival. One may get an idea of the possible size of governmental subsidies from the fact that industrial export subsidies for 1966 are estimated at approximately IL55 million.[4] The overall cost of unrecovered capital is probably a great deal higher, and as suggested in Chapter 2 the silent partner, the government, usually ended up carrying the burden of risky ventures and helped prolong them via subsidies. It is even harder to say with any degree of accuracy what the opportunity costs of this capital might have been. An analysis of every alternative to the unsuccessful investments would have to be made.

It was suggested earlier that the major decisions affecting the future of a firm and whether it will be conventionally successful or subsidy dependent are jointly reached by the firm representatives (consultants or executives) and the relevant government authority in charge of the particular subsidy. It was stated that the absentee investor is largely removed from the decision-making domain. But it is significant to note that while the interests of the absentee investor are promoted and defended by the class of consultants and executives described in this chapter, a new participant in the decision process has emerged. This new partner in the decision process is the government personified by the various bureaucrats in charge

of subsidy approval and distribution. These government representatives are involved in practically all major decisions related to the establishment of the subsidized firm (location,
technology, product, and market) and, at a later stage, in
various decisions affecting the daily operations of the firm.
Thus, in reality, the subsidy-maximizing firm becomes to a
large extent a centrally operated company, and the government
officials responsible for the allocations of subsidies become
"program managers." Although they may not be aware of the
fact that they carry out managerial functions, these officials
are nonetheless aware of their power and seek to expand it
both in the firm, through active participation in the decision
process, and in the government by a perpetuation of the subsidy system.

This new level of management is well received by the
subsidy-maximizing firm since it will ensure the continuous
inflow of subsidy benefits. On the other hand, the conventionally successful firm will be deterred by this phenomenon.
This deterrence is caused by the fact that these government
officials usually lack experience and expertise in industrial
management, and their evaluations and subsequent decisions
are not necessarily based on cost-effectiveness considerations
so vital to a successful organization. As for the subsidy-maximizing firm, with its built-in inefficiency and managerial incompetency, a lack of experience in cost-effectiveness considerations can be an added blessing.

NOTES

1. M. Spencer and N. Siegelman, Managerial Economics:
Decision-Making and Forward Planning (Homewood, Ill.:
Richard D. Irwin, 1964).

2. M. Bentov, "Technology Determines the Output,"
Economic Quarterly, 53 (Tel Aviv, June, 1967).

3. See Bank of Israel, "Changes in the Financial Structure
of Israel's Industrial Companies, 1956/57 to 1961/62," Bank
of Israel Bulletin, 19 (Jerusalem, May, 1963).

4. Ibid.

CHAPTER **6** CHARACTERISTICS
OF THE SUBSIDY-
MAXIMIZING FIRM

The preceding analysis of the impact of government subsidies on industrial management decisions indicated that subsidies can alter such decisions. Uneconomical investments
will be made, inferior locations will be chosen, and capital-
intensive methods of production will be preferred under the
subsidy impact. Such decisions lead to the creation of a new
phenomenon; namely, the subsidy-maximizing firm, the rationale of which has been described in the previous chapter. This
rationale, while not necessarily consistent with the accepted
decisions criteria of the conventional profit-maximizing firm,
is nevertheless a built-in element of unique characteristics'
structure of the subsidized firm.

It seems appropriate to conclude this volume of the impact
of government subsidies on industrial management with the
following summary of characteristics of the subsidy-maximizing
firm. These characteristics are based upon the data and analysis presented throughout the entire investigation, and will not
only give further insight into the behavior of the subsidy-maximizing firm, but will also enable us to evaluate the social and
economic impact of this phenomenon.

PURPOSE AND GOALS

Profit

The subsidized industrial firm seeks the optimization of
its profits. But this "profit" includes the subsidy factor and
hence is not necessarily commensurate with the accepted criterion of profit maximization of the nonsubsidized firm where
profit is construed as a function of sales and the overall operational efficiency of the firm. This profit is derived from the
maximization of subsidies received.

Survival

The subsidized industrial firm has a built-in higher probability for survival due to vested government interests developed through the subsidy programs which serve as a prime
incentive in the considerations to continue financial support of
the firm thereby prolonging its life, while nonsubsidized firms
would probably be doomed under similar conditions. The existence of a built-in higher probability of survival alters management's motivations and goals as compared to the management of nonsubsidized firms where survival is a primary
consideration.

Government Relations

The significant effect of existing government vested interests in the subsidized firm makes the continuation and maintainance of good relations with government authorities a company
goal in its own right.

MANAGERIAL AND
ORGANIZATIONAL CHARACTERISTICS

Managers

In countries where subsidies are a prime factor in the
decision to establish or continue the operations of a firm,
there seems to exist a preference to draw the firm's executive
cadre from exgovernment officials, especially from those who
have held positions which have brought them into frequent contacts with authorities connected with the granting of subsidies.
This is consistent with the trend to employ consultants with
similar background, and facilitates the emergence of a new
type of investor--the subsidy manipulator absentee owner.

Management Costs

With the government in the role of a silent partner whose
financial participation is nevertheless high in proportion to
equity capital, the door is open for management costs
relatively higher than those in the nonsubsidized firm. This

characteristic is true for both the owner-manager combination
and the employed executive. The former by enlarging his own
compensations seeks quicker and larger returns on the portion
of capital that he had invested while the latter is in many cases
compensated not necessarily for his excellence in managing
the firm but for the proximity and effectiveness in developing
and maintaining the necessary relations with relevant government authorities.

Administrative Versus Production Costs

The maintainance of close ties with government authorities
necessitates the type of executive above. In many cases the
productivity of such executives is measured by the number and
frequency of company-government communications. This in
turn calls for expanded administrative and clerical work to
cope both with the obtainment of subsidies and the necessary
follow-up of established executive-government officials relationships. Consequently, in conjunction with the trend towards
capital-intensive operations and the applicability of Parkinsonian
laws, the A/P ratio for both personnel and costs will tend to
be higher in the subsidized industrial firm.

FINANCIAL CHARACTERISTICS

Capital Structure

A direct result of increased government subsidies such
as cash grants, direct loans, and guarantees for loans is the
high-debt equity ratio of the subsidized firm. In many cases
the ratio may be as low as 70 percent to 75 percent of the total
investment capital.

Loan Guarantees

Both the subsidy programs and the subsequently derived
government vested interest in the firm results in the continuous
availability of partial government guarantees for borrowing,
otherwise a major financing problem for nonsubsidized firms.

Future Cash Flows

The availability of both subsidies and partial government
guarantees for borrowing largely reduces the risk of future
cash flows thereby reducing the significance of a major factor
in capital budgeting considerations in the nonsubsidized firm.

Extra Subsidy Financing

Should a subsidized firm require capital in excess of what
it is able to obtain through the various subsidy programs for
the purpose of paying the interest on loans, it will experience
high cost of capital for such extra subsidy financing.

Return on Equity Investment

While return on the total investment of the subsidized firm
may be relatively low, at the same time the returns on equity
investment will be comparatively higher.

Capital Budgeting

Characteristics examined in the sections Capital Structure
and Loan Guarantees above cause managements of subsidized
firms to exhibit a bias towards short payback projects to permit a quick recovery of equity investment. This in turn leads
to the acceptance of higher risk investments.

OPERATIONAL CHARACTERISTICS

Lead-Time for Establishment

Since the period between the conception of the investment
idea and the start of production is utilized for financial manipulations with the available subsidies, management will seek to
extend the time interval between the investment proposal and
approval to actual manufacturing. Consequently subsidized
firms will exhibit a longer time-lead for establishment and
beginning of operations.

Plant Location

Wherever management decides to locate in a particular
region to take advantage of certain location-inducing subsidy
programs they will nevertheless follow accepted location criteria and establish themselves on sites where the combination
of factors makes them nearest to the ideal location under non-
subsidy conditions. This leads to a concentration of subsidized
firms close to the perimeter dividing the nonsubsidized from
the subsidized region. In such locations subsidized firms
exhibit temporary lower break-even points for the duration of
the subsidy program and usually higher break-even points
caused by the comparative location disadvantages when the
subsidy program is terminated.

Plant Building and Facilities

One of the common subsidies is government participation
in plant building. In many cases the government will provide
the land and the building according to management specifications and at other times it will bear a major portion of building costs. Consequently newly erected subsidized plants will
be more spacious, luxurious, and costlier. This in turn leads
to both the availability of unutilized floor space and higher costs
of maintenance while at the same time increasing flexibility
for layout and future expansion. The latter are derived advantages for an optimistic forecast of the company's operations.

Process-Technology Characteristics

Grants and low-interest loans for the acquisition of machinery and equipment have the effect of lowering the relative
machine-labor cost ratio thereby leading management to become biased towards a capital-intensive process and hence a
higher level of technology. Similar to characteristics described
in the section on Plant Location, which showed an underutilization of available space, the purchase of special purpose equipment when not necessarily justified by demand conditions causes
the subsidized industrial firm to exhibit productive capacity
underutilization or high equipment idle time.

Product Choice

The existence of product- or industry-oriented subsidies automatically creates a bias for the selection of such products or industries should a potential investor have no preset preference as to the product he wants to manufacture or the industry in which he wants to be. Frequently companies with established products will seek to introduce also the subsidized product so that the entire company may benefit from the individual product incentives. In such cases the search for alternative new product lines is reduced to the feasible few on the subsidy program list.

Production Run

The large set-up costs usually associated with the transition from one product to another whenever special purpose machines are utilized leads to long production runs which in turn result in high inventories and storage costs.

Overall Operational Efficiency

The sum of the characteristics listed thus far--under-utilized space, unused capacity, higher maintenance costs, extensive machine idle time, and high inventory costs--combine to characterize the subsidized firm with a low overall operational efficiency.

MARKETING CHARACTERISTICS

Sales Forecast

Wherever the government in addition to subsidizing the firm becomes also its client a guaranteed market for a portion of the firm's output is created which reduces the uncertainty in sales forecasts and consequently increases the certainty of projected revenues.

Market Targets

In their allocation of market targets subsidized firms will show distinct preference for those markets with higher subsidy rates, for example, export subsidies. The choice of market targets will subsequently influence product choice and will affect the relevant decisions of advertising and distribution channels.

Promotion Costs

An extensive utilization of government participation in the promotion expenses allows the subsidized firm to reduce the budget usually allocated for such purposes and channel these funds to areas where a more immediate and direct revenue may be attained.

Choice of Projects

It may be generalized that subsidized firms will show an inclination towards government-oriented projects consistent with the other relevant characteristics enumerated thus far.

ENVIRONMENTAL RELATIONS

Community Relations

Because of the government's vested interests in the subsidized firm it is conceivable that authorities would be restrained in exerting pressure on the firm to show greater sensitivity and to take responsible attitudes and positive action in matters of major interest to the community such as pollution, unemployment, and education.

Government Influence

The continuous reliance and dependence of subsidized companies on the carefully nurtured relations with government officials, and the knowledge that the fate of these subsidies is entirely at their discretion makes these subsidized companies

susceptible to pressure to conform to and be sympathetic with
government policies that a nonsubsidized company has the freedom to repudiate.

Government Control

The various officials responsible for the allocation of subsidies inadvertently carry out major managerial functions and
are instrumental in critical areas of decisions directly affecting subsidized industrial firms. Thus such firms become
partners in the government centrally controlled operation.

This list of characteristics is by all means not exhaustive
and a careful observation of the day-to-day operations of a
subsidy-maximizing firm would reveal additional relevant
characteristics. Nevertheless the characteristics listed thus
far provide us with a better understanding of the goals and behavior of such firms as contrasted to the aspirations and behavior of conventional profit-maximizing firms. This in turn
may serve as a criterion to management in its decision to pursue the road that leads to becoming a subsidy-dependent firm,
while at the same time it may extensively aid governments in
the formulation of subsidy policies and in the design of efficient
follow-up techniques to ensure the effectiveness of various
subsidy programs.

BIBLIOGRAPHY

BIBLIOGRAPHY

BOOKS

Aharoni, Y., The Foreign Investment Decision Process,
Division of Research, Boston: Graduate School of Business
Administration, Harvard University, 1966.

Amsterdam-Rotterdam Bank, Commerce and Industry in the
Netherlands: A Base for Business Operations in Europe,
Amsterdam, 1967.

Bach, G. L., Economics: An Introduction to Analysis and
Policy, 4th ed., Englewood Cliffs, N. J.: Prentice-Hall,
1965.

Banco Exterior De Espana, Foreign Investment in Spain,
Madrid, 1963.

Bank of America National Trust and Savings Association, Focus
on Taiwan: An Economic Study of the Republic of China,
New York, 1968.

Bank of Israel, Annual Report 1966, Jerusalem, May, 1967.

Barish, N. N., Economic Analysis for Engineering and Managerial Decision-Making, New York: McGraw-Hill, 1962.

Brittenden, F. H., A Guide to Investment Grants, London:
Butterworth, 1966.

Central Bureau of Statistics, Statistical Abstract of Israel
1967, 18, Jerusalem, 1968.

Centro De Estudios Economicos Del Sector Privado, Manual
De Disposiciones Sobre Fomento Industrial, Mexico
District Federal, 1969.

Chemical Bank of New York Trust Company, International Economic Survey--Taiwan, New York, 1966.

China Productivity and Trade Center, Pamphlet, Taipei, October 31, 1967.

Dean, J., Managerial Economics, Englewood Cliffs, N. J.: Prentice-Hall, 1962.

Department of Investment Promotion and Supplies, Guide to Investment in Pakistan, Karachi: Government of Pakistan Press, 1964.

Drucker, P. F., Managing For Results: Economic Tasks and Risk-Taking Decisions, New York: Harper & Row, 1964.

Eckaus, R. S., "The Factor-Proportions Problem in Under-developed Areas," in The Economics of Underdevelopment, ed. A. N. Agarwala and S. P. Singh, New York: Oxford University Press, 1968.

Eckstein, O., Public Finance, Englewood Cliffs, N. J.: Prentice-Hall, 1967.

Economic Planning Authority, Israel's Economic Development: Past Progress and Plan for the Future, Jerusalem, March, 1968.

Economic Planning Board, Questions and Answers: A Guide for Foreign Investors, Seoul, 1967.

_____, Office of Investment Promotion, Investment Guide to Korea, Seoul, 1967.

_____, Foreign Capital Inducement Law, Seoul, 1967.

Embassy of Brazil, Survey of the Brazilian Economy, Washington, D. C., 1966.

Export Promotion Bureau, Annual Report 1966-1967, Karachi, 1968.

Foreign Capital Research Society, Japanese Industry, Tokyo, 1968.

Fredrickson, B. E., ed., Frontiers of Investment Analysis,
    Scranton, Pa.: International Textbook Company, 1965.

Friedman, M., Capitalism and Freedom, Chicago: University
    of Chicago Press, 1965.

Galbraith, J. K., The Affluent Society, Boston: Houghton-
    Mifflin, 1958.

_____, The New Industrial State, Boston: Houghton-Mifflin,
    1967.

Greenhut, M. L., Plant Location: In Theory and in Practice,
    Chapel Hill: University of North Carolina Press, 1956.

Hirsch, S., The Export Potential of Israeli Manufacturing
    Enterprises, Tel Aviv: Israel Management Institute, 1968.

Hoover, E. M., The Location of Economic Activity, New York:
    McGraw-Hill, 1948.

Horie, Y., The State and Economic Enterprise in Japan,
    Princeton: Princeton University Press, 1965.

Industrial Development and Investment Center, A Brief Report
    on the Supply of Labor in Taiwan, Taipei, 1967.

_____, Statute for Technical Cooperation, Taipei, 1966.

Johnson, H. G., Economic Policies Toward Less Developed
    Countries, New York: Frederick A. Praeger, 1967.

Lösch, A., The Economics of Location, New York: John
    Wiley and Sons, 1967.

Manne, A. S., ed., Investment for Capacity Expansion: Size,
    Location, and Time-Phasing, Cambridge: The M.I.T.
    Press, 1967.

Marglin, S. A., Public Investment Criteria, Cambridge: The

    M.I.T. Press, 1967.

Melman, S., Decision-Making and Productivity, New York:
    John Wiley and Sons, 1957.

_____, Dynamic Factors in Industrial Productivity, New York: John Wiley and Sons, 1956.

Ministry of Commerce and Industry, Surveys of Israeli Industries, prepared for the Economic Conference of April, 1968, Jerusalem, February, 1968.

Ministry of Finance, Foreign Capital Investment in Spain-- Rules and Regulations, Madrid, 1963.

Myint, H., The Economics of Developing Countries, New York: Frederick A. Praeger, 1964.

Nwogugu, E. I., The Legal Problems of Foreign Investment in Developing Countries, Manchester, G. B.: Manchester University Press, 1965.

Organization for Economic Cooperation and Development, Fiscal Incentives for Private Investment in Developing Countries, Paris, 1965.

Patinkin, D., The Israeli Economy in the First Decade, A Falk Institute Report, Jerusalem, 1959.

Porterfield, J. T. S., Investment Decisions and Capital Costs, Englewood Cliffs, N. J.: Prentice-Hall, 1965.

Rautenstrauch, W. and Villers, R., The Economics of Industrial Management, 2nd ed., New York: Funk and Wagnalls, 1957.

Sapir, P., The Three E's: Efficiency, Employment, Export, 1967/68 Budget Address, December 20, 1966, Jerusalem: Government Press, 1967.

Shoup, C. S., Public Finance, Chicago: Aldine, 1969.

Singer, H. W., International Development: Growth and Change, New York: McGraw-Hill, 1964.

Spencer, M. and Siegelman, N., Managerial Economics: Decision-Making and Forward Planning, Homewood, Ill.: Richard D. Irwin, 1964.

_____, Government Incentives, Jerusalem, 1968.

_____, Israel Investment Authority Operations to December 31, 1965, Jerusalem, January, 1966.

_____, Israel Investment Authority Report to December 31, 1966, Jerusalem, 1967.

_____, Israel Investment Authority Report for 1967, Jerusalem, January, 1968.

State of Israel Investment Authority, Israel Investors' Manual, Jerusalem, 1968.

_____, Law for the Encouragement of Capital Investment, Jerusalem, January, 1967.

U. S. Arms Control and Disarmament Agency, Economics Bureau, World Military Expenditures and Related Data, Research Report 68-52, Washington, D. C.: U. S. Government Printing Office, December, 1968.

U. S. Congress, House, 1969 Listing of Operating Federal Assistance Programs Compiled During the Roth Study, Washington, D. C.: U. S. Government Printing Office, 1969.

U. S. Congress, Joint Economic Committee, Subsidy and Subsidy-Effect Programs of the U. S. Government, Joint Committee Print, Washington, D. C.: U. S. Government Printing Office, 1965.

U. S. Department of Commerce, "Establishing a Business in Peru," Overseas Business Report, Washington, D. C.: U. S. Government Printing Office, October, 1966.

ARTICLES

Banco Central de Reserva Del Peru, Economic and Financial Review, Lima, November/December, 1965.

Bank of Israel, "Changes in the Financial Structure of Israel's Industrial Companies, 1956/57 to 1961/62," Bank of Israel Bulletin, 19, Jerusalem, May, 1963.

_____, "The Financial Structure of Israel's Industrial Companies," Bank of Israel Bulletin, 17, Jerusalem, January, 1963.

Bentov, M., "Technology Determines the Output," Economic Quarterly, 53, Tel Aviv, June, 1967.

Bruno, M., "Productivity and Rates of Return in Israel 1952/61," Economic Quarterly, 37/38, Tel Aviv, March, 1963.

Goodrich, C., "State In, State Out--A Pattern of Development Policy," Journal of Economic Issues, II, 1, December, 1968.

Halevi, N., "Economic Policy Discussion and Research in Israel," The American Economic Review, September, 1969.

Hertz, D.B., "Risk Analysis in Capital Investment," Harvard Business Review, January-February, 1964.

McLean, J.G., "How to Evaluate New Capital Investments," Harvard Business Review, November-December, 1968.

"Proper Site Selection--Part III," Duns Review, 85, 1965.

Stobaugh, R.B., "Where in the World Should We Put That Plant?", Harvard Business Review, January-February, 1969.

Thomson, J.H., "The Community Subsidy to Industry," Business Horizons, Spring, 1963.

ABOUT THE AUTHOR

Nachum Finger is Assistant Professor of Organization and Management at the Graduate School of Business Administration, Rutgers University. In addition to teaching, Professor Finger is actively engaged both in research and as an Industrial and Management Engineering Consultant to industry.

Dr. Finger received his B.S., M.S., and Eng. Sc. D. from Columbia University.